LTL 5/04

ALLEN COUNTY PUBLIC LIBRARY

3 1833 04630 4736

P9-EEC-898

ALLEN COUNTY PUBLIC LIBRARY

P9-EEC-898

ULTIMATE
BREAD

ULTIMATE
BREAD

ERIC TREUILLE & URSULA FERRIGNO

Photography by
IAN O'LEARY

LONDON, NEW YORK, MELBOURNE,
MUNICH, and DELHI

US TEAM
SENIOR EDITOR Barbara Berger
RECIPE CONSULTANTS Wesley Martin
Barbara Bowman, Gourmetsleuth
EDITORIAL CONSULTANT Jane Perlmutter
DTP DESIGNER Milos Orlovic
EDITORIAL ASSISTANT Phil Poyer

UK TEAM
MANAGING EDITOR Stephanie Farrow
DTP DESIGNER Sonia Charbonnier
PROJECT EDITOR Julia Pemberton Hellums
SENIOR EDITOR Nicky Graimes
EDITOR David Summers
PROJECT ART EDITORS Hilary Krag, Gurinder Purewal
SENIOR MANAGING EDITOR Krystyna Mayer
MANAGING EDITORS Mary Ling, Susannah Marriott
MANAGING ART EDITOR Toni Kay
DTP DESIGNER Karen Ruane
PRODUCTION MANAGER Maryann Webster.

Second American Edition 2004
2 4 6 8 10 9 7 5 3 1

Published in the United States by
DK Publishing Inc.,
375 Hudson Street, New York, New York 10014

Copyright © 2004 Dorling Kindersley Limited
Text copyright © 1998 Eric Treuillé and Ursula Ferrigno

All rights reserved under International and Pan-American Copyright
Conventions. No part of this publication may be reproduced, stored in a
retrieval system, or transmitted in any form or by any means, electronic,
mechanical, photocopying, recording or otherwise, without prior written
permission of the copyright owner. Published in Great Britain by
Dorling Kindersley Limited

DK Publishing, Inc. offers special discounts for bulk
purchases for sales promotions or premiums. Specific, large-quantity needs can
be met with special editions, including personalized covers, excerpts of existing
guides, and corporate imprints. For more information, contact:
Special Markets Department,
DK Publishing, Inc.,
375 Hudson Street, New York, NY 10014
Fax: 212-689-5254

Cataloging-in-Publication Data
is available from the Library of Congress

ISBN 0-7566-0370-6

Color reproduction in Italy by GRB
Printed and bound by L. Rex Printing Company Ltd, China.

Discover more at
www.dk.com

CONTENTS

INTRODUCTION

In France and in Italy, where we come from, a meal is not a meal without bread. There, bread is taken very seriously. The daily visit to the bakery is a ritual that punctuates the rhythm of life. People choose their bread with special care and patronize the baker of their choice with an almost religious allegiance. It is said that the table is not set until bread is put on it. Bread is used to eat *with* as much as it is eaten: a piece of bread is used as a kind of secondary fork, and then is used to wipe the plate clean of every last morsel. Indeed, for many, culinary life begins with bread as mothers give their babies a hard crust on which to cut their teeth.

All over the world, bread plays an important role in festivals and celebrations, traditions, and superstitions. Eric's father, like others of his generation, still marks the sign of the cross with the tip of his knife on the base of a loaf before he cuts it. Both of us clearly remember being warned as children not to place a loaf of bread top crust down on the table because it was sure to bring bad luck.

We were privileged that our first experiences of making bread came early. Indeed, Eric's first contact with professional cooking was with bread; during his school vacations, he worked as a *mitron*—baby baker—at Le Fournil, his uncle's *boulangerie* in southwestern France. Ursula remembers the hot summer evenings when her grandmother would light the wood-fired oven on the terrace of their family home in Campania. She recalls the sweet, yeasty fragrance of the seemingly magically growing dough and its soft, springy texture as she formed it into a round, for it was a family tradition that each person shape and top his or her own pizza.

When work drew us away from our homes to London, we were puzzled and shocked at the acceptance of mass-produced, inferior bread. It was our natural appreciation of bread with which we were raised that propelled us into baking bread at home for ourselves and then into teaching others how to do the same. Besides providing good food, breadmaking enlivens both your kitchen and your life when it becomes a regular activity. We hope that this book brings the same tremendous pleasure and satisfaction.

Eric   Ursula

THE FUNDAMENTALS OF BREADMAKING

MAKING BREAD REQUIRES little more than a pair of hands, an oven, and patience. The recipe for success is simple: time and warmth are all it takes to transform a few basic ingredients into a springy, silky dough that bakes to a crackly, crusted loaf. It is like most things— easy when you know how, with practice making perfect. If we had to choose one single phrase that we feel is essential to breadmaking, it would be this: *bread is alive*. It is a living, growing entity and, above all, the product of its ingredients and its surroundings; it responds, just as we do, to its environment—"treat rising dough as if it were human" advises an old English farmhouse cookbook. While we advocate the use of scales, timers, and thermometers, remember that observation is the baker's traditional tool. The more you make bread, the better your bread will be. Your mistakes are rarely irreversible (*see pages 162–163* for problem solving) or inedible.

ESSENTIAL INGREDIENTS AND TECHNIQUES

Flour is the main ingredient of most breads, accounting for about three-quarters of the finished loaf. The flour you choose will give your bread its individual character. Mass-produced, highly refined brands will make an honest loaf, but we urge you to seek out organic flours from independent mills to experience the taste and texture of truly great homemade bread.

The choice of flour affects not only the quality of the baked bread but also the breadmaking process. Flour will absorb more, or less, liquid depending on the variety of wheat that it was made from, the place where it was harvested, and the way in which it was milled. Such variables are compounded by the humidity in the air—on a damp day, flour will absorb less liquid than on a dry one. The quantities of liquid given in the recipes can never be more than guidelines. Our mixing technique (*see pages 44–45*) suggests that you hold back a proportion of liquid and add it as needed. This method acts as a safeguard against overly wet dough and the consequent need to add extra flour, which upsets the balance among flour, salt, and yeast.

If you require a little more liquid than stated in the recipe, do not hesitate to add it; your aim is to produce a dough conforming to the consistency specified in the recipe, be it firm, soft, or wet. Observing and understanding the condition of your dough, and what it requires, is the key to successful breadmaking.

THE IMPORTANCE OF TEMPERATURE

A warm kitchen is a perfect place for making bread. Ideally, ingredients should be at room temperature before mixing—except the yeast, which should be dissolved at body temperature, 98.6°F. A summer heat wave or a cool pantry must be brought into the equation, and you may find it necessary to use cooler or warmer water to correct the balance—keeping in mind that yeast is killed by temperatures over 130°F.

In the days before central heating, people used to take their dough to bed with them! Less eccentric rising spots during cold weather include a warm bathroom, an oven with the pilot light on, and a position near, but not too close to, a radiator, an open fire, or a stove. Choose a glass or plastic bowl for rising dough; metal conducts heat too efficiently, and you may find the dough rising unevenly and drying on the side closest to a nearby heat source. Use temperature to control the baking timetable. Decrease the water temperature and leave the dough in a cool spot in order to slow down the rising process to fit in with your schedule; the refrigerator is ideal for all-day or overnight rising. Remember to allow several hours for the dough to return to room temperature (*see page 50*).

THE JOYS OF BREADMAKING

Breadmaking works miracles on all levels. The slow, rhythmic kneading is therapeutic, opening up the lungs and rib cage and releasing stresses and strains with gentle efficacy. Watch as the warmth and pressure of your hands bring the yeast to life and transform a few commonplace ingredients into a growing dough. Everybody loves the smell of bread that is being made. The yeasty fragrance of the rising dough permeates the kitchen, only to be superseded by the delicious aroma of the bread baking. Enjoy the process of breadmaking as well as the results.

BAKING AT HIGH ALTITUDES

Altitudes above 3,500ft have low atmospheric pressure, which causes bread dough to rise and proof more quickly than is indicated in the book's recipes. No adjustments are needed to the ingredients, but keep an eye on the dough and do not allow it to increase in volume more than is specified.

Breads that rise too quickly will not develop. To prevent this, allow the dough to rise twice (*see page 50–51*) before shaping.

At altitudes over 3,000ft, increase the baking temperature by 59°F. This extra heat is needed to help form the crust in the initial stages of baking and to prevent the bread from over-rising during its final minutes in the oven.

SUCCESSFUL BREADMAKING

The golden rule for measuring all baking ingredients is to choose one system and use it for the entire recipe.

All spoon measurements are level: 1 teaspoon equals ⅙fl oz; 1 tablespoon equals ½fl oz. All eggs used in the book are large unless otherwise specified. Unsalted butter should always be used for breadmaking unless otherwise specified.

Make sure that all the ingredients used are at room temperature; be sure to take eggs, butter, and milk out of the refrigerator in sufficient time.

A GALLERY
OF BREADS

A WORLD OF POSSIBILITIES IS REVEALED IN THIS

GALLERY OF BREADS, WHICH CELEBRATES A

TRULY UNIVERSAL FOOD. A MEAL IS NOT A MEAL WITHOUT

BREAD IN COUNTRIES AS DIVERSE AS ITALY, INDIA, MEXICO,

AND FRANCE. A VARIETY OF TEXTURES AND TASTES ABOUNDS

TO DEFINE THIS GLOBAL CULINARY STAPLE. ILLUSTRATED

HERE IS A SELECTION OF BREADS FROM SOME OF THE

WORLD'S MOST FAMOUS BREADMAKING TRADITIONS.

 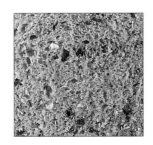 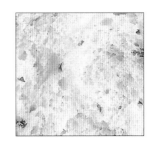

FRENCH BREAD

18TH-CENTURY FRENCH BAKER KNEADS DOUGH IN A WOODEN TROUGH

BREAD IS AT THE HEART of the French culinary experience, and once even defined social status—the long, elegant white *Baguette* was affordable only to stylish city dwellers, and rustic breads, like *Pain de Campagne*, were staples of life in the country. Today, however, these country-style sourdough breads have captured the imagination of contemporary bakers from New York to Tokyo.

COURONNE

Bread shapes in France were often designed by the baker to satisfy the needs of his customers; the hole in the middle makes the loaf easy to carry over the arm like a shopping basket. As well as being practical, the loaf's shape increases the proportion of crust to crumb. *Recipe page 85.*

PAIN DE SEIGLE

In France, rye bread originated in mountainous regions, like the Pyrenees and the Vosges, where it was a staple bread. Today, it is more often served in Parisian brasseries, thinly sliced and thickly buttered as an accompaniment to oysters. *Recipe page 93.*

PISTOLETS

These distinctively shaped rolls are traditional to Belgium and northeastern France, where they are a Sunday breakfast treat. The characteristic indentation along the top of each roll is easily made with the handle of a wooden spoon. *Recipe page 79.*

PAIN DE CAMPAGNE

Made throughout France in innumerable shapes and sizes, *Pain de Campagne* varies by region as well as by baker. All country breads have a thick, dark crust liberally dusted with flour, giving them their characteristic two-tone appearance. *Recipe page 85.*

FOUGASSE

One of the 13 desserts traditional to a Provençal Christmas, *Fougasse* can now be bought all year round. This decorative branch-shaped bread is flavored and enriched with olive oil. Tasty ingredients are often added to the bread dough—crisp bacon, chopped anchovies, or caramelized onions are very popular. *Recipe page 149.*

BAGUETTE

A crackly golden crust and light chewy interior are the signatures of this world-renowned classic bread. The French say it is better to buy two loaves at a time because one is always half eaten by the time it arrives home. *Recipe page 79.*

PAIN TORDU

From the Limousin, a rural region in the center of France, *le tordu*, the "twist," is a popular shape. It is favored by bread connoisseurs who prize crust as highly as crumb. *Recipe page 85.*

ITALIAN BREAD

16TH-CENTURY VENETIAN BAKERY

AN ITALIAN TABLE is not dressed without bread. Renaissance paintings depict tables adorned with baskets of freshly baked bread, and this appealing image is just as current today. Each region of Italy has its own distinctive style of cooking and breadmaking. The food of northern Italy is very rich, and its ingredients reflect the historical wealth of this area. Delicate, light breads are made here. Southern Italian food is the food of a humbler people, and a luscious bread filled with cheese and vegetables serves as a meal in itself.

STROMBOLI

This southern Italian bread is stuffed with mozzarella, fresh herbs, and shallots. During baking, the generous filling erupts out of the indentations made in the bread's crust. Hence it is named after the volcanic island off the coast of Sicily. *Recipe page 106.*

SCHIACCIATA CON L'UVA

This Tuscan bread is made to celebrate the grape harvest. It is filled with wine-soaked raisins from the previous year's harvest and traditionally topped with the new season's grapes. *Recipe page 109.*

PANE DI RAMERINO

Enriched with olive oil and eggs, studded with raisins, and scented with fresh rosemary, this delicious bread is most commonly seen at the Tuscan breakfast table. *Recipe page 115.*

GRISSINI TORINESI

From the city of Turin, these crispy breadsticks can be made as thin as a pencil or as fat as a cigar. Toppings vary from simple coarse salt to the seed or dried herb of your choice. *Recipe page 80.*

CIABATTA

Distinctive to the Emilia Romagna region of Italy, *Ciabatta* is now baked around the world. It was created as a light, airy textured bread to accompany the region's rich pasta and meat dishes. *Recipe page 90.*

BRITISH BREAD

**BAKING DAY IN A
19TH-CENTURY ENGLISH VILLAGE**

WHATEVER THE SHAPE, the typical British loaf has a soft, tender crumb and a crispy rather than crusty exterior, often liberally dusted with flour. Through the centuries, the unerring preference of the British people has been for loaves made with white wheat flour. Historically, fine white bread graced only the tables of the lords of the manor. There were separate guilds for bakers of white and brown breads, and the saying "to know the color of your bread" meant to know your place in society.

VICTORIAN MILK BREAD

Milk is an important ingredient in many British breads. The use of milk in place of water softens both the crumb and the crust. This bread has a velvety texture and a golden smooth exterior. Its fancy scroll shape is typical of the popular Victorian novelty breads. *Recipe page 76.*

BLOOMER

Half milk and half water are used to make this long, plump loaf, with its crispy crust and light, tender crumb. A typically British shape, this deeply scored loaf dramatically expands, or "blooms," when baked. *Recipe page 76.*

COTTAGE LOAF

The most distinctive British shape, the Cottage Loaf, is made by stacking a small round loaf on top of a larger round and joining them by making a deep impression, traditionally formed with the baker's elbow. *Recipe page 73.*

GRANARY PAN LOAF

Granary bread is made with a blend of wheat and rye flours mixed with malted grains. It is the most recent addition to the family of British breads; its slightly sweet, nutty taste and moist texture make this loaf a favorite of both children and adults. *Recipe page 73.*

SCOTS BAPS

Baps are soft, flat rolls found all over Great Britain but are mostly associated with Scotland. There they are traditionally eaten at breakfast and called morning rolls or buns. *Recipe page 77.*

IRISH SODA BREAD

This everyday Irish bread is traditionally "baked" in a cast-iron pot set over the embers of an open fire. With a cakelike texture, this bread is made without yeast and is best eaten on the day it is baked. *Recipe page 141.*

17

EUROPEAN BREAD

**19TH-CENTURY
GERMAN BAKERY**

THE BREADS OF EUROPE fall into two categories – the hearty country breads eaten daily and the lighter, richer, more refined breads reserved for feasts and celebrations. The traditional country breads were rarely made with wheat flour alone but incorporated a common staple of the region: rye in Germany, corn in Portugal, and potatoes in Hungary. Wheat flour was an expensive and precious commodity, and these healthful additions provided nourishing bulk to the everyday European loaf.

PULLA

This saffron-colored, cardamom-scented bread wreath is the traditional Christmas loaf of Finland. No longer restricted to festive occasions, *Pulla* is now baked and eaten all year long. *Recipe page 150.*

LANDBROT

The name of this crusty rye bread translates literally as "bread of the land," and is one of the few breads baked throughout Germany—a rarity in this intensely regional country that boasts 400 kinds of bread. *Recipe page 92.*

BROA

Originally from the Minho Province in the north of Portugal, this corn bread is now eaten all over the country. Corn grows profusely in Portugal and is used in many of the native dishes. *Recipe page 78.*

HUNGARIAN POTATO BREAD

In Hungary, potatoes are a staple commodity. This traditional bread uses potatoes to add moisture and substance to the loaf, which is subtly spiced with aromatic caraway seeds. *Recipe page 103.*

PARTYBROT

Guests can help themselves to this inviting German bread. It serves as the perfect centerpiece to a party's buffet table. *Recipe page 120.*

AMERICAN BREAD

**18TH-CENTURY
COLONIAL BAKER**

PIONEERS AND HOMESTEADERS who settled North America brought with them the breadmaking traditions of their native countries and adapted them to suit the rustic conditions of their new home. Without the system of communal bakeries that had existed in Europe since the Middle Ages, they established an important tradition of home baking that still exists. North America is famous for its unique sourdoughs and quick breads, which are made without the traditional yeast leavens.

SAN FRANCISCO SOURDOUGH

The origins of this bread date back to California's gold rush. Prospectors carried with them, in a package strapped to their waists, a mixture of flour and water that fermented to produce a leaven for this chewy, tangy bread. *Recipe page 86.*

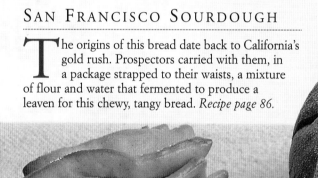

FAN TANS

Native to New England, these fancy shaped rolls also go by the name Yankee Buttermilk. They have a light and airy texture that complements a hearty stew or roast. *Recipe page 121.*

PARKER HOUSE ROLLS

Soft rolls are a Sunday dinner staple all over America. This unique shape was created and popularized by the Parker House hotel in Boston during the late 19th century. *Recipe page 118.*

CINNAMON RAISIN BREAD

Enriched with milk and flavored with an inner whirl of raisins, this bread is an all-American breakfast favorite. Served toasted and topped with butter and cinnamon sugar, it is a fond childhood memory. *Recipe page 123.*

CORN STICKS

A heavy skillet was used by early settlers to cook corn bread on the hearth. Here, the batter is baked in a cast-iron mold that forms this quick-bread batter into small ears of corn. *Recipe page 142.*

EASTERN BREAD

MEALTIMES IN THE MIDDLE EAST ALWAYS INCLUDE BREAD

THE IMPORTANCE OF BREAD in the Middle East cannot be overstated. In the Arab world, bread is revered as a gift from God and the staff of life itself. Honor is asserted with the vow "on my family's bread, I swear to tell the truth"; contentment expressed by the saying "his water jug is filled, and his bread is kneaded." Bread is eaten at every meal, from the simplest snack to the grandest banquet, and indeed takes the place of cutlery throughout the region. The most common bread is flat with a hollow pocket in the middle, used for filling with salads, grilled meats, or any of the region's mouthwatering *mezze*.

LAVASH

It is said that *Lavash* originated in Armenia, but it is also eaten throughout Lebanon, Turkey, and Syria. Rolled paper-thin, it is traditionally cooked in a large outdoor oven called a *tannur*. *Recipe page 134.*

PIDE

Recognized by its distinctive ridged pattern, golden crust, and topping of nigella seeds, *Pide* is traditionally prepared for the Muslim festival of Ramadan, when it is eaten to break the fast at sunset. It can be topped with fennel seeds instead of nigella seeds. *Recipe page 137.*

BARBARI

This light, crusty Persian bread, when topped with cheese and fresh herbs, is commonly served for breakfast in Iran. When made with water instead of milk and sprinkled with sugar instead of seeds, the bread becomes a much-loved children's snack called *shirmal*. *Recipe page 136.*

PAIN TUNISIEN

With a tender crumb and crisp crust, this bread is made with semolina flour. Semolina is produced from durum wheat—a staple of North Africa that is widely used to make bread and couscous, a cracked grain. *Recipe page 135.*

PITA

This soft, oval- or round-shaped bread with a pocketlike hollow in the middle is made all over the region, where it also goes by its Arab name of *khubz*. *Recipe page 134.*

FESTIVE BREAD

**PREPARING BREAD FOR A
17TH-CENTURY FESTIVITY**

THE CUSTOM OF BAKING SPECIAL BREADS to serve at festive celebrations and on religious holidays is an ancient one. In contrast to the plain, hearty loaves that define the traditional "daily bread," festive breads are usually made with the most expensive and highly prized ingredients—golden butter and eggs, aromatic spices and flavorings, and sweet dried and candied fruits. These ceremonial breads are formed into traditional shapes that have special symbolic meanings. Some are now commonly served throughout the year and not just for an occasion.

PANETTONE

This rich, golden loaf from Milan is studded with golden raisins and delicately perfumed with citrus peel. Its dome-shaped top is said to resemble the cupolas of the churches of its native Lombardy. *Panettone* is traditionally enjoyed at Christmas. *Recipe page 155.*

PAN DE MUERTO

Flavored with orange and anise, this sweet bread is baked on the Mexican Day of the Dead, when families honor their dead by visiting the graves with offerings of flowers and food. *Recipe page 152.*

BOLO-REI

Rich breads and cakes are traditional in southern Europe to celebrate the feast of the Epiphany, on January 6. This lavishly decorated Kings' Cake from Portugal is shaped to symbolize the crowns of the Three Kings, who arrived in Bethlehem on this day. *Recipe page 154.*

CHALLAH

The golden braided loaf traditional for the Jewish Sabbath is the most familiar shape. It is shown here coiled into a circle to symbolize continuity and baked to celebrate the Jewish New Year, Rosh Hashanah. *Recipe page 150.*

BAKING ESSENTIALS

FLOUR, WATER, AND YEAST – THESE ARE THE ESSENTIAL INGREDIENTS OF BREADMAKING. WHEN BROUGHT TOGETHER WITH THE HELP OF YOUR HANDS, A FEW BASIC TOOLS, AND A HOT OVEN, THEY CAN BE TRANSFORMED INTO A WARM, FRAGRANT LOAF. THE BAKING ESSENTIALS ILLUSTRATED IN THIS SECTION REVEAL WHAT BREAD IS: A FEW SIMPLE INGREDIENTS ELEVATED BEYOND THEIR HUMBLE ORIGINS TO BECOME AN EVERYDAY MIRACLE.

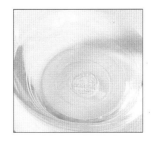

WHEAT FLOURS

FLOUR IS A KEY INGREDIENT in all breads. Wheat flour is by far the most common type used in breadmaking. The wheat kernel consists of three parts: bran, germ, and endosperm. The wheat bran is the husk that encloses the kernel, while the nutritious wheat germ is the seed of the future plant. The endosperm, the inner part of the kernel, is full of starch and protein. This high protein content makes wheat ideal for breadmaking. When dough is kneaded, the protein in the flour develops into gluten, an elastic substance that traps the carbon dioxide generated by the leavening agent, allowing the dough to rise.

THE MILLING PROCESS

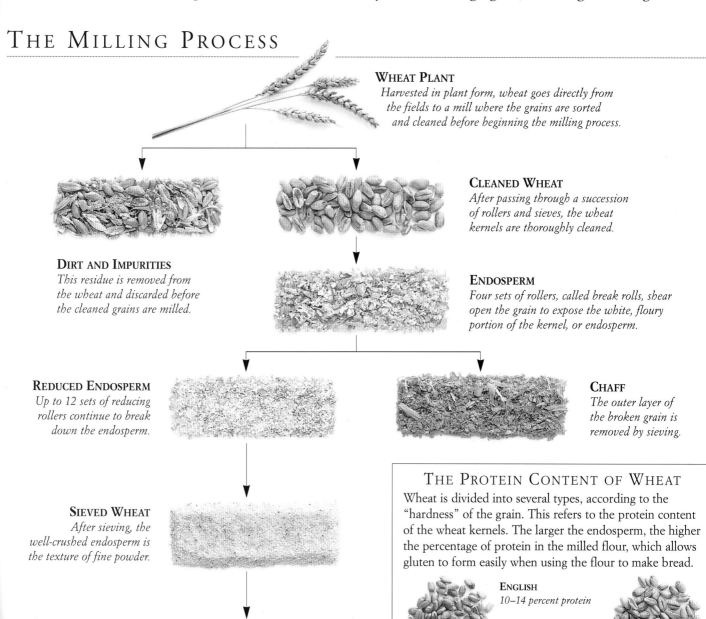

WHEAT PLANT
Harvested in plant form, wheat goes directly from the fields to a mill where the grains are sorted and cleaned before beginning the milling process.

CLEANED WHEAT
After passing through a succession of rollers and sieves, the wheat kernels are thoroughly cleaned.

DIRT AND IMPURITIES
This residue is removed from the wheat and discarded before the cleaned grains are milled.

ENDOSPERM
Four sets of rollers, called break rolls, shear open the grain to expose the white, floury portion of the kernel, or endosperm.

REDUCED ENDOSPERM
Up to 12 sets of reducing rollers continue to break down the endosperm.

CHAFF
The outer layer of the broken grain is removed by sieving.

SIEVED WHEAT
After sieving, the well-crushed endosperm is the texture of fine powder.

THE PROTEIN CONTENT OF WHEAT
Wheat is divided into several types, according to the "hardness" of the grain. This refers to the protein content of the wheat kernels. The larger the endosperm, the higher the percentage of protein in the milled flour, which allows gluten to form easily when using the flour to make bread.

ENGLISH
10–14 percent protein

NORTH AMERICAN
10–18 percent protein

FLOUR
Sieving and reduction continue until the type of flour desired is obtained.

TYPES OF WHEAT FLOUR

ALL-PURPOSE FLOUR
This multipurpose flour, produced from a blend of hard and soft wheat, can be used for bread and pastries but contains less protein and gluten than bread flour made for breadmaking.

WHOLE-WHEAT FLOUR
Made from the complete wheat kernel, this flour makes a fuller flavored, nutritious but denser loaf than all-purpose flour. The extra bran hinders rising.

BREAD FLOUR
This flour is milled from hard wheat and has a higher proportion of gluten than all-purpose flour. This ensures an elastic dough and a lighter loaf.

COARSE SEMOLINA FLOUR
This coarse, gritty flour is milled from the endosperm of durum wheat, which is one of the hardest varieties of wheat. Use it in combination with all-purpose flour for making bread.

FINE SEMOLINA OR DURUM FLOUR
Also referred to as semola di grano duro, *this high-gluten flour is made from the endosperm of durum wheat and is ground twice to produce a fine texture that makes it ideal for breadmaking.*

GRANARY FLOUR
A combination of whole-wheat, white, and rye flours mixed with soft malted grains, this flour makes a textured loaf with a nutty, naturally sweet flavor. It is found in specialty shops.

BROWN FLOUR
This flour contains most of the wheat grain's germ but has had some of the bran removed. Therefore, it produces a lighter loaf than does whole-wheat flour.

MIXING FLOURS

Experimenting with different combinations of wheat and nonwheat flours enables the home baker to create breads with special textures, flavors, and colors. The secret of mixing flours successfully is balance. See the selection of nonwheat flours on pages 30–31 and follow the guidelines given here to get the best results when combining flours:

Any mixture must always include some wheat flour. The protein content of wheat flour allows the development of gluten, which is critical for a well-risen bread.

Two-thirds bread flour combined with one-third nonwheat flour gives bread optimum volume and texture.

The greater the proportion of nonwheat to wheat flour, the more pronounced its effect on the flavor and texture of the bread.

If the proportion of nonwheat to wheat flour is increased, the dough will rise more slowly, creating a much denser loaf.

Different flours absorb water at varying rates. Sift flours together to ensure an even distribution before adding liquid to them.

NONWHEAT FLOURS

FOR CENTURIES, VARIOUS DRIED GRAINS and roots have been ground and used to make bread. Most flours and meals—including those made from rye, oats, barley, and corn—are ground from the seeds of cereal plants. The seeds vary in shape and size, but all have a structure similar to that of the wheat kernel and are ground in the same manner. These flours produce breads with different flavors, textures, and nutritional values. Wheat flour, with its high gluten content, is preferable for risen breads. Low-gluten and nongluten flours must be mixed with at least 50 percent wheat flour to make a properly risen bread, but the addition of a few tablespoons of one of these flours will deepen a bread's flavor.

PRINCIPAL CEREAL GRAINS

RYE PLANT

GRAIN   FLOUR

RYE
Ground from cleaned grains, rye flour inhibits gluten development. Even a small addition, mixed with wheat flour, adds a distinctive tang to bread. Dark rye flour contributes a strong flavor, while light rye flour is milder and paler.

OAT PLANT

GROATS   PINHEAD OATS   FLOUR

OATS
Oats that have been cleaned and hulled are called groats. Pinhead oats are groats that have been cut into several pieces. Oat flour is ground from groats and is gluten-free. It adds rich flavor and texture to a bread.

BARLEY PLANT

PEARL BARLEY   FLOUR

BARLEY
Barley seeds with the bran removed are called pearl barley, which is eaten in soups and stews. Barley flour is ground from pearl barley and is gluten-free. Mixed with wheat flour, it adds a sweet, earthy flavor.

CORN PLANT

KERNELS   COARSE MEAL   FINE MEAL

CORN
Dried corn kernels are ground into three textures of meal—coarse, medium (called polenta), and fine. All are gluten-free and have a distinctive corn flavor.

LOW-GLUTEN AND NONGLUTEN FLOURS

PEOPLE WHO ARE INTOLERANT of wheat or gluten can use low- or nongluten flours to make bread. However, since it is gluten that gives dough its elasticity and strength and allows it to rise, breads made exclusively with the flours shown here and opposite may have a dense, crumbly texture. When used in combination with wheat flour, these flours will contribute extra nutritional value and flavor to a bread. See page 29 for tips on mixing wheat and nonwheat flours.

SPELT FLOUR
A flour rich in nutrients with a slightly nutty flavor, spelt is low in gluten, but high in protein. This makes it a digestible substitute for wheat flour in breadmaking for the gluten-intolerent.

MILLET FLOUR
Millet flour is low in gluten, but very rich in protein, vitamins, and minerals, with a distinctively sweet flavor. It is used mostly in combination with wheat flour for bread.

BROWN RICE FLOUR
Milled from the whole rice grain, brown rice flour is gluten-free. When blended with wheat flour, it contributes a dry texture and a sweet, nutty taste to a bread.

POTATO FLOUR
This gluten-free flour is made from cooked, dried, ground potatoes. Used mostly as a thickener, when combined with other flours, it produces a moist crumb in breads.

CHICKPEA FLOUR
Made from ground chickpeas, this flour is gluten-free. Just a small proportion gives a rich flavor to leavened flat breads and other savory dishes.

QUINOA FLOUR
Quinoa contains more protein than any other grain as well as all eight essential amino acids. It is gluten-free and when mixed with wheat flour is a rich source of nutrients for bread.

CORNMEAL FLOUR
Most commonly used in American quick and nonyeast breads, this gluten-free flour can be combined with wheat flour to make bread with a gritty, coarse texture and a sweet, corn flavor.

BUCKWHEAT FLOUR
Buckwheat flour is ground from the seeds of a plant native to Russia that is not akin to the wheat plant, and is gluten-free. This gray-brown flour has a distinctively bitter flavor.

INGREDIENTS

BREADMAKING involves just a few simple ingredients, all of equal importance. Leavens cause a dough to rise by creating bubbles that expand the gluten strands in the dough. This is not possible without the presence of liquid, which transforms the flour and yeast into a dough. Sugar encourages the dough to rise, while salt inhibits the process. Enrichments—such as butter, oil, and eggs—allow the baker to vary a bread's flavor, texture, and appearance.

LEAVENS

YEASTS

YEAST IS THE COMMONLY USED LEAVEN in breadmaking. It is a living organism that converts the natural sugars in flour to gases. Cake yeast is available from the bakery section of most supermarkets. It should be used within 1–2 days of purchase, since its freshness can be unreliable. Dry and instant yeast are more concentrated and long-lasting; use by their expiration date.

CHEMICAL LEAVENS

WHEN MOISTENED with liquid, baking powder and baking soda instantly create air bubbles, which act as the leaven in a quick bread batter. This requires the loaf to be baked immediately. Cream of tartar is used in combination with baking soda.

BAKING POWDER

BAKING SODA

CREAM OF TARTAR

DRY YEAST
Activate in lukewarm water before adding to the flour.

CAKE YEAST
Dissolve in lukewarm water before adding to the flour.

INSTANT YEAST
Sprinkle into the flour; activate by adding liquid.

CHEMICAL LEAVENS
These leavens are used as the rising agents in the Quick Bread recipes (see pages 138–145).

LIQUIDS

WATER
The primary liquid used to dissolve yeast and to form a bread dough.

MILK
Creates a tender crumb when used in place of water.

LIQUID IS FUNDAMENTAL to breadmaking. Liquid activates the yeast when it is at the correct temperature, and it gives life to the flour by transforming it into a dough. For a loaf with a very tender crumb, water can be replaced with milk. Buttermilk and yogurt can be used interchangeably to produce a bread with a moist, almost cake-like texture. Extra liquid can be added to a dough when it is needed to achieve the dough consistency specified in a recipe.

YOGURT
Adds a tangy flavor and a moist texture to a bread.

BUTTERMILK
Can be made from skim milk and lemon juice (see page 164).

SALTS

SALT IS USED in most bread recipes to control the rate of fermentation and to add flavor. The presence of salt in a dough inhibits fermentation, which strengthens the developing gluten. This results in a bread with a stable crumb, a long shelf life, and more taste than breads made without it.

FINE SALT
Dissolves well and is best for making bread dough.

COARSE SALT
Sprinkled over an unbaked loaf, this makes a flavorful topping.

ENRICHING INGREDIENTS

FATS ARE THE PRIMARY enriching ingredients that when used in a bread recipe change the character of the resulting dough. The fat coats the gluten strands, creating a barrier between the flour and the yeast, which slows down both the fermentation and the rising time. In a recipe calling for a large amount of fat, the enriching ingredient or ingredients will be incorporated into the dough after an initial period of rising. In general, breads made with enrichments have a soft, tender crumb and become more cakelike the higher the proportion of butter and eggs added. Select only the best-quality enrichments for breadmaking.

VEGETABLE OIL
Use a light, neutral oil like sunflower.

BUTTER
Use only unsalted butter when enriching a bread dough.

SUGARS

SUGAR CAN ACCELERATE the fermentation process of bread dough by providing additional food for an active yeast culture. However, modern yeasts do not need sugar to become active. Sugar is no longer a necessary ingredient in bread recipes, but it is used to enhance a bread's flavor, texture, and crust color.

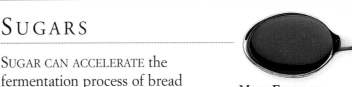

MALT EXTRACT
Made from malted wheat or barley, this encourages active yeast.

MOLASSES
Adds a sweet, slightly bitter flavor and a dark golden color to bread.

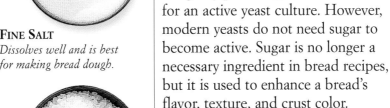

GRANULATED SUGAR
The most commonly used sugar for making bread.

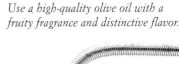

HONEY
Honey melts well when used for making bread.

OLIVE OIL
Use a high-quality olive oil with a fruity fragrance and distinctive flavor.

EGGS
Choose fresh eggs with undamaged shells for making enriched doughs.

EQUIPMENT

THE EQUIPMENT AND TOOLS required for breadmaking are as simple as the essential ingredients. The basic equipment needed to make most of the breads in this book includes an accurate scale, a measuring cup and spoons, a large glass bowl, a wooden spoon, a dish towel, a baking sheet, a sharp blade, and an oven.

The remaining equipment shown will help you tackle additional skills and special recipes. Be sure that you have a large, clean surface to work on that allows you plenty of room to move around; a marble slab, plastic board, or wooden table is best. Although a bare countertop is also fine, avoid tiles because the dough can stick to the grout.

MEASURING

BREADMAKING SHOULD BEGIN with careful measuring. For the best results, it is essential that the ingredients are in correct proportion to one another. When following a recipe, it is important to use one system of measurement, either nonmetric or metric, throughout. These are not interchangeable systems. Before using the scale, check that the needle is on zero when it is empty. Never measure dry or wet ingredients over the mixing bowl. When using a measuring cup, always bend down to pour the liquid at eye level.

MEASURING CUP
A cup with clearly marked units is important for measuring liquids.

MEASURING SPOONS
Always level off ingredients in measuring spoons.

SCALE
An accurate scale is essential for weighing small amounts.

MIXING AND RISING

CHOOSE GLASS OR PLASTIC bowls and wooden spoons for breadmaking. Metal bowls and spoons react with yeast, creating a metallic aftertaste in a batter. It is also advisable to avoid letting dough rise in metal bowls since they conduct heat, causing dough to rise too quickly. To prevent a dry crust from forming on a dough, cover the bowl with a clean dish towel during rising and proofing.

WOODEN SPOON
Essential for mixing batter.

GLASS JAR
Useful for making and storing sourdough starters (see page 43); they should not be sealed.

DISH TOWELS
Use to cover doughs during rising and proofing and to wrap soft-crusted breads warm from the oven.

GLASS BOWLS
These offer an all-around view and withstand vigorous use.

OTHER HELPFUL TOOLS

PASTRY SCRAPER
*A pliable, plastic scraper is ideal
for handling sticky dough.*

PASTRY BRUSH
*An all-purpose
boar-bristle brush
is best for applying
glazes and washes.*

SCALPEL
*Use to slash
the top of a
risen dough
before baking
(see page 62).*

SCISSORS
*Kitchen scissors
can be used to
create decorative
slashes in dough
(see page 62).*

THERMOMETER CASE

**INSTANT-READ
THERMOMETER**
*Practical for checking water
temperature when preparing
yeast (see page 41).*

STRAINER
*A stainless-steel strainer is
best for sifting flours together.*

ROLLING PINS
*Wooden cylindrical
rolling pins are best
for shaping dough.*

BREAD KNIFE
*A serrated knife will penetrate a hard
crust and slice through bread cleanly.*

APPLIANCES

ELECTRICAL EQUIPMENT can be
useful for mixing and kneading
bread doughs. While a food
processor ensures thorough
mixing and partial kneading
of a dough, a heavy-duty mixer
allows a baker to develop the
full elasticity of a dough
through constant kneading
for a longer period of time.
However, electric mixers and
processors can overwork and
overheat the dough when set
on a high speed. See pages
66–67 for tips on how best
to use them.

FOOD PROCESSOR

HEAVY-DUTY MIXER

BAKING

AFTER THE INGREDIENTS have been carefully measured and mixed to the proper consistency, the final stages of breadmaking also require the same careful attention. Preheat the oven in advance and use an oven thermometer to check its accuracy. A kitchen timer allows you to keep track of the baking time, as well as the rising and proofing times. Thicker baking pans and trays are best, since they resist buckling in the oven at high heats and prevent loaves from burning on the bottom.

KITCHEN TIMER
A clearly marked kitchen timer with a loud alarm will ensure accurate baking, rising, and proofing times.

OVEN THERMOMETER
A thermometer will detect any variations in oven temperature (see page 64).

LOAF PAN
Pans made of medium-weight metal are most frequently used in this book.

CORN STICK PAN
Each depression in this cast-iron pan shapes a single serving of corn bread.

WATER SPRAYER
A fine-spray nozzle is advisable for adding moisture to the oven while a bread is baking. Avoid spraying the oven light or heating elements directly (see page 63).

TERRA-COTTA TILES
Tiles help radiate heat evenly and retain moisture in the oven, producing superior, thick-crusted, free-form breads (see page 63).

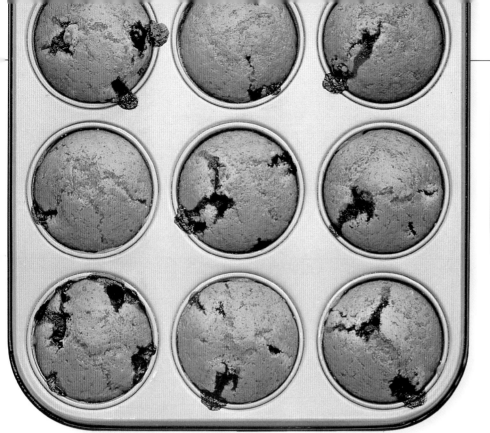

MUFFIN TIN
Use a muffin tin with a nonstick surface and deep cups for muffin recipes.

BREAD BOARD
Wooden boards are best for slicing bread because they are kind to the serrated blade of a bread knife.

BAKING SHEET
Use a heavy-duty, nonflexible, metal baking sheet for free-form loaves and rolls.

BRIOCHE MOLDS
The sloping sides of these classic molds induce a maximum final rise and height during baking.

WIRE RACK
Use a wire rack to cool breads in order to prevent a soggy bottom crust (see page 65).

FRENCH BAGUETTE TRAY
This perforated tray ensures an even heat throughout baking, resulting in a crisp, golden outer crust.

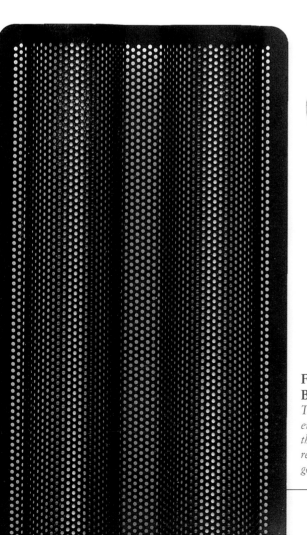

BASIC TECHNIQUES

T HE BASIC TECHNIQUES OF MAKING BREAD ARE

NOT COMPLICATED OR DIFFICULT TO FOLLOW.

SUCCESSFUL BREADMAKING, HOWEVER, REQUIRES TIME

AND PATIENCE—TRY NOT TO RUSH EACH STAGE. USE

THIS SECTION TO LEARN ABOUT, FEEL, AND OBSERVE THE

PROCESSES THAT TRANSFORM BASIC INGREDIENTS

INTO A FINISHED LOAF. THIS IS YOUR HANDIWORK;

THE JOYS OF MAKING YOUR OWN BREAD BEGIN HERE.

HOW TO BEGIN

RECISE PROPORTIONS and accurate quantities of leavening, water, and flour form the foundation on which all good bread is based. The rising agent, or leaven, is the key to transforming simple ingredients into a risen bread. In this book, yeast, in either dry or cake form, is the most commonly used leaven.

Yeast is a living organism that feeds on the sugar and starch present in flour to live and grow. The yeast produces carbon dioxide as it grows: this gas causes the bread dough to rise. Once activated in water, yeast will live for 15 minutes before it must be added to flour, the food source it requires to stay alive.

MEASURING THE INGREDIENTS

ACCURACY IS CRUCIAL when making bread. Measure all the ingredients carefully before you begin. Follow either nonmetric or metric measurements throughout the recipe. These two types of measurement are not interchangeable. For nonmetric, measure by cup, tablespoon, or teaspoon.

With flour and other dry ingredients, level the top. For metric, use a clearly marked scale to weigh dry ingredients. With liquid ingredients, put a measuring cup on a flat surface and bend down so that the measure mark is at eye level.

PREPARING THE YEAST

BOTH DRY AND CAKE YEAST must be dissolved in lukewarm water to activate. This should be done just before adding the yeast to the flour. Avoid using metal bowls or utensils to prepare the yeast. Metal can impart an unpleasant aftertaste to a yeast mixture.

PREPARING INSTANT YEAST

TO USE INSTANT YEAST, sprinkle it directly onto the flour. The yeast will activate once the liquid has been added. The standard method of mixing the dough must be followed, since the sponge method (*see page 44–45*) cannot be used with instant yeast.

PREPARING DRY YEAST

1 Sprinkle dry yeast granules into a small glass bowl containing lukewarm water; let it dissolve for 5 minutes.

2 Once the yeast has dissolved, stir the mixture with a wooden spoon. The yeast mixture is now ready to be added to the flour.

Granules will float on the surface and then sink

Foam indicates that the yeast has been activated

PREPARING CAKE YEAST

1 Use a wooden spoon to crumble the cake yeast in a small, glass bowl and add the water to it. As a general rule, the amount of water added to dissolve the yeast will be about a quarter of the water specified in the recipe.

2 Use a wooden spoon to cream the yeast until it dissolves in the water and forms a smooth, thoroughly blended paste. The yeast mixture is now ready to be added to the flour.

WATER TEMPERATURE

The ideal temperature for preparing yeast is 98.6°F. The easiest method for achieving this is to mix two-thirds cold tap water with one-third boiling water. Lukewarm water should be comfortable to the touch, not too hot, but not cool. An instant-read thermometer is a fail-safe method for checking the water temperature (*see page 35*).

As a living organism, yeast is very sensitive to temperature. The temperature of the liquid you use to dissolve the yeast and to make the dough is crucial: too hot, and the yeast is killed; too cool, and its growth is inhibited.

Cool water can be helpful when conditions in the kitchen are extremely warm and you wish to slow down the rising process. Adding cool water to the yeast will inhibit the rate of fermentation, allowing the bread to rise at a normal rate when the room temperature is above normal.

USING A STARTER

STARTERS OFFER AN ALTERNATIVE METHOD of preparing the yeast before mixing the bread dough. A portion of the yeast is prepared and then combined with water and flour. This mixture is then left to ferment for between two hours and five days, which results in a finished bread with an open, airy texture and a superior flavor. Breads made with a starter require planning because additional time is needed to allow the starter to ferment. Once the starter has fermented, it is ready for the mixing step (*see pages 44–45*). The main difference between the main starter methods described here is time; the ingredients are the same—flour, water, and yeast.

MAKING A STARTER

ANY BREAD CAN BE MADE with a starter. Simply mix some of the flour, water, and yeast together into a thick batter, and let it ferment at room temperature. The proportions of ingredients and the timing depend on the recipe. The timing varies from two hours for a French *poolish* to thirty-six hours for a fully matured Italian *biga* (*see page 84*).

1 In a nonmetalic bowl, combine the amount of flour, water, and prepared yeast specified in the recipe. Mix with a wooden spoon to form a thick, yet pliable, batter.

The mixture should be thick but not too stiff

2 Cover the bowl with a dish towel, and let the starter ferment at room temperature for the amount of time specified in the recipe. The mixture will begin to bubble and have a mild yeasty fragrance.

3 The starter is now ready to be mixed with the remaining ingredients. Add the starter and dissolved yeast to the well formed in the flour. Mix the ingredients as directed in the recipe (*see pages 44–45*).

CREATING AND FEEDING A SOURDOUGH STARTER

A TRADITIONAL SOURDOUGH STARTER is made with a flour and water paste that is left to ferment by wild airborne yeast. Here some yeast is added to encourage the fermentation process. Once established, a sourdough starter can be kept indefinitely in the refrigerator. The longer a starter is kept, the better the flavor of the baked bread. If you do not make bread regularly, it is important to "feed" the starter every two weeks. To do this, stir, discard half, and replace with an equal amount of water and flour.

1 In a large glass jar, sprinkle or crumble the yeast into the water; let it dissolve for 5 minutes. Stir in the amount of flour specified in the recipe. Cover the jar with a dish towel and ferment at room temperature for at least 48 hours and up to 5 days. The starter will become a loose, frothy batter. Use immediately or refrigerate for up to 2 weeks.

The fermented starter is ready to use when it has become a loose batter

2 After using a portion of the starter, replace it with an equal amount of flour and water to keep it active for the next time you make bread. For example, if the recipe calls for 1 cup starter, after removing this amount stir 1 cup flour and ½ cup water back into the jar. Ferment at room temperature for 12–24 hours before refrigerating.

OLD-DOUGH METHOD

A piece of "old dough" can also be used as a leavening agent. Instead of making a flour and dissolved yeast batter, simply incorporate a piece of dough saved from a previous batch of plain bread into your new batch. Old dough can be made from scratch (*see page 86*) and kept wrapped in the refrigerator for up to two days before using or freezing. Alternatively, when making a plain bread remove a walnut-size piece of dough after the rising period. Wrap the dough loosely in waxed paper and foil, allowing room for it to expand, then refrigerate or freeze it. To use the dough, if frozen, thaw it in the refrigerator overnight, then let it rest at room temperature for a minimum of two hours.

Wrapped properly, old dough will keep in the freezer for up to 6 months

MIXING

THE PRIMARY OBJECTIVE of mixing is to combine the basic ingredients into a soft, pliable consistency ready for kneading. The quantity of liquid required will often vary, depending on the type of flour used as well as the level of humidity and temperature on the day of breadmaking. A little less, or a little more, liquid than the recipe states may be required. Add extra liquid 1 tablespoon at a time; it is better to err on the side of too soft than too dry. Take note of the consistency of the dough described in each recipe, and add additional liquid accordingly. The sponge method adds a period of fermentation (specified in the recipe) to mixing. This results in a bread with a lighter crumb and a less yeasty flavor. Techniques for mixing added ingredients into the dough are illustrated in the recipe section.

1 In a large bowl, combine the flour and salt. Use a wooden spoon to form a well. Add the dissolved yeast and any starter (*see pages 42–43*) to the well. If the recipe requires the ingredients to "sponge," refer to the method illustrated below.

2 Using a wooden spoon, draw in the flour from the sides of the bowl, a little at a time, to combine with the dissolved yeast in the well. Proceed to step 3, opposite. ▶

SPONGE METHOD

FOLLOW STEP 1, above, then draw enough of the flour from the sides of the bowl into the liquid to form a soft paste (*see left*) when mixed thoroughly.

COVER THE BOWL with a dish towel and leave for 20 minutes, or longer if specified in the recipe, until the paste is frothy and has expanded slightly in volume (*see left*). Proceed to step 3, opposite. ▶

3 Gradually pour in half of the remaining liquid while mixing in the flour from the sides of the bowl. As the water is added, the texture of the combined ingredients will change from a crumbly mixture to a shaggy, slightly sticky mass that will begin to come away from the sides of the bowl and form a ball (*see below*). Add the rest of the water, as needed, to achieve the consistency specified in the recipe. The dough should remain soft and not too dry before it is transferred to a floured surface to knead (*see pages 46–47*).

KNEADING

SSENTIAL FOR AN OPEN-TEXTURED, full-flavored bread, kneading performs a crucial function in preparing the dough to rise. First, it completes the mixing process by distributing the activated yeast throughout the dough. Continued kneading then allows the flour's proteins to develop into gluten, which gives dough the ability to stretch and expand.

Starches are broken down to feed the yeast, which creates bubbles of carbon dioxide. These bubbles cause the dough to rise. The actions shown are a guide to kneading a basic dough. Specific instructions, such as how to knead a soft, wet dough (*see page 88*) or how to knead coarse ingredients into a dough (*see page 99*), are demonstrated in the recipe section.

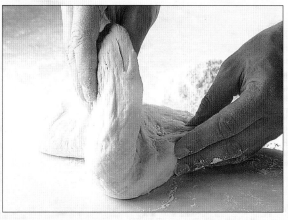

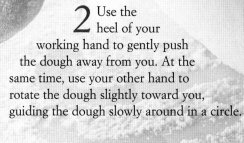

1 Shape the dough to begin kneading by folding one half over the other, bringing the top half toward you. Keep a little additional flour on the side to lightly dust the dough as you knead should it become difficult to handle. Use this extra flour sparingly.

2 Use the heel of your working hand to gently push the dough away from you. At the same time, use your other hand to rotate the dough slightly toward you, guiding the dough slowly around in a circle.

3 Repeat these kneading actions, gently folding, pushing, and rotating the dough continuously for approximately 10 minutes, or until the dough achieves a firm touch, a silky smooth surface, and an elastic texture. Take time to work the dough slowly and firmly, but do not use excessive force. The dough will gradually become more elastic and easier to knead. Shape the dough into a ball for rising (*see pages 50–51*).

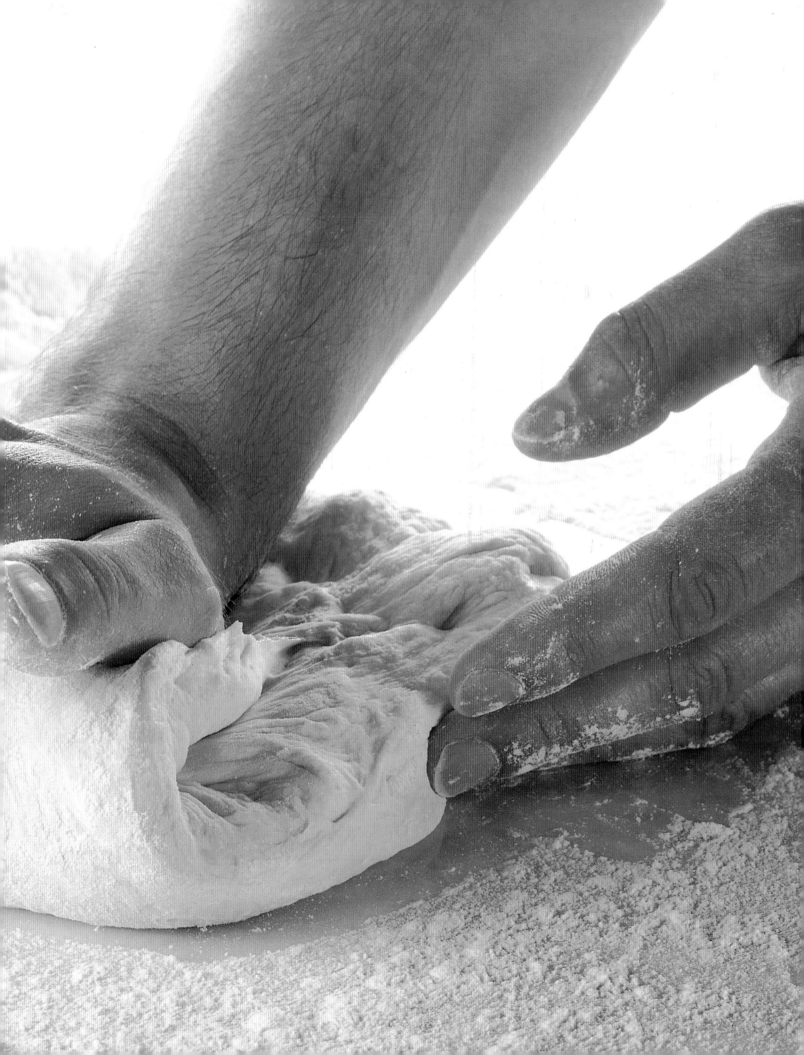

USING APPLIANCES

A FOOD PROCESSOR or heavy-duty electric mixer can be used as an alternative to mixing and kneading bread dough by hand. When using a food processor, check the capacity of your machine and, if necessary, divide the ingredients evenly so you can mix and knead the dough in batches. Some kneading by hand will also be necessary. Bread dough can be made entirely in a heavy-duty electric mixer by using the mixing paddle to mix and the dough hook to knead. Be careful not to overwork the dough —high speeds stress the dough, causing it to rise incorrectly. Make use of the pulse button or low-speed setting on each appliance.

USING A FOOD PROCESSOR

1 Before starting, always fit the machine with a plastic dough blade. A metal blade will stress and overheat the dough.

2 Put the flour and any other dry ingredients into the work bowl; pulse to mix. With the machine running, pour in the dissolved yeast, followed by half the remaining liquid. If using a starter, as specified in the recipe, add it to the work bowl at this point.

3 Add the rest of the water and continue to run the machine until the dough starts to form into a ball. Then let the dough rest in the machine for 5 minutes. Process the dough to knead for another 45 seconds. Turn out onto a lightly floured work surface and continue to knead by hand until smooth and elastic, about 3–5 minutes. Let the dough rise (*see pages 50–51*).

The dough should be firm and sticky before kneading by hand

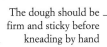

— HANDY TIPS —

• *Use slightly cool water to dissolve the yeast to counterbalance the heat generated by the machine.*

• *When preparing the dough in batches, turn them out onto a lightly floured work surface. Knead them together to form one piece of dough. Continue until smooth and elastic.*

• *Use the pulse button to prevent the machine from overheating the dough. Do not run the machine continuously for more than 30 seconds at a time.*

USING A HEAVY-DUTY MIXER

1 Dissolve the yeast or make a starter, as specified in the recipe, and place directly in the mixing bowl. Use the paddle attachment to mix in half the flour on low speed, then add the remaining liquid ingredients to the bowl.

2 Once the mixture forms into a loose batter, remove the paddle. Replace it with the dough hook. Add the remaining dry ingredients gradually to the mixer.

3 Continue adding the dry ingredients until the dough pulls away from the sides of the bowl. Increase the speed to medium and work the dough until smooth and elastic, about 8–10 minutes. If the dough climbs up the hook, stop the machine, push it back down, and continue. Remove the dough from the mixing bowl to rise (*see pages 50–51*).

The dough will collect around the hook as it is kneaded

— HANDY TIPS —

• *Use only an electric mixer with a proper dough hook for kneading. A mixer with only paddle and whisk attachments is not equipped for breadmaking.*

• *An electric mixer is particularly helpful for kneading very stiff doughs as well as doughs with enrichments and flavorings added to them.*

• *Check the recipe for the dough consistency required. Add extra water, if needed, 1 tablespoon at a time.*

RISING & PUNCHING DOWN

THE SPEED OF RISING depends on certain factors, such as temperature and humidity, as well as on the integral elements of a recipe, such as the type of flour and the method of leavening (that is, with or without a starter). On a warm, humid day, dough should rise more quickly than on a cold, dry one. However, the exact effect of temperature can be difficult to predict. Rising times become more predictable only after years of experience with the same bread recipes. The novice baker might find it difficult to tell when the dough has doubled in size; use the test described in step 3 to help check the progress. If the dough over-rises, see page 163 for a remedy.

RISING

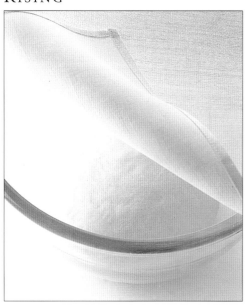

1 Place the kneaded dough in a lightly oiled glass or ceramic bowl large enough to allow the dough to double in size. Metal containers should be avoided since they can conduct heat, causing the dough to rise too quickly. Cover the bowl with a dish towel and let it rise in a cool to normal, draft-free room.

RISING THE DOUGH IN THE REFRIGERATOR

This method allows breadmaking to be split into two stages, and is therefore useful for those with busy schedules. Place the dough in a deep glass bowl that will allow it to expand, brush with oil, and cover tightly with plastic wrap. To achieve a complete rise, refrigerate for at least eight hours. After rising, remove from the refrigerator. Leave it at room temperature for two hours before shaping.

2 Allow the dough to rise until doubled in size. For most doughs, this will take 1–2 hours. Whole-wheat breads and enriched breads will take longer to rise. The slower a dough rises, the more chance there is for it to develop flavor and texture. Do not allow the dough to over-rise.

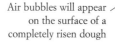
Air bubbles will appear on the surface of a completely risen dough

3 To ensure that rising is complete, test the dough by gently pressing with a fingertip. When rising is complete, the indentation made will spring back gradually. If the dough is under-risen, the indentation will spring back at once. If the dough is over-risen, the finger will create a permanent mark that will not spring back at all (*see page 163*).

PUNCHING DOWN

ONCE THE DOUGH HAS RISEN completely, punch down or deflate the dough by pressing down with your knuckles as demonstrated. Turn the dough out of the bowl onto a lightly floured work surface.

CHAFING

FORM THE DOUGH into a ball by cupping your hands gently around it. Apply a light downward pressure to the sides, while simultaneously rotating the dough continuously in a steady clockwise motion. Continue until the dough is formed into an even round shape. This action is called chafing. Some recipes specify an extended chafing time at this point. Otherwise, allow the dough to rest for 5 minutes and then proceed to the shaping step.

Cup the dough gently
with your hands

SHAPING & PROOFING

AFTER THE DOUGH IS PUNCHED DOWN and has rested, it is ready to be shaped. The techniques on the following six pages illustrate how to form the basic loaf shapes that are most frequently called for in the recipe section. Each stage of the shaping process requires careful attention—handle the dough gently and avoid overshaping or excessive reshaping. Apply pressure evenly and allow the dough to rest if it begins to resist or tighten. Transfer the shaped loaf to a prepared baking sheet to proof (*see page 57*). Proofing allows the dough to rise for a final time before baking. Avoid over-proofing the dough; use the recommended test to check the progress.

MAKING A LONG LOAF

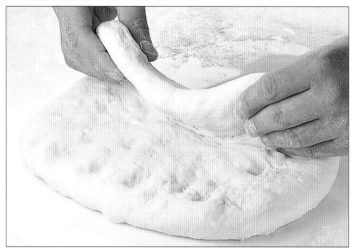

1 Flatten the dough with the lightly floured palm of your hand to expel any gas bubbles. Keep the dough in a round shape by exerting pressure evenly. Take one end of the dough and fold it into the center. Press gently to seal the fold.

2 Fold the other half of the dough into the center, so the folds overlap along the middle of the loaf. Gently press along the seam with the lightly floured palm of your hand to seal the two folds.

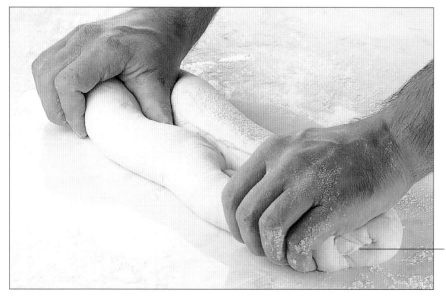

3 Use the thumbs of both hands to create an indentation in the center of the dough. Before bringing the top half toward you, rest your fingertips along the top of the dough and give a firm, short push forward. This action tightens the interior of the dough and gives an even-textured crumb when the bread is baked.

Press down into the center of the dough and fold one half over the other

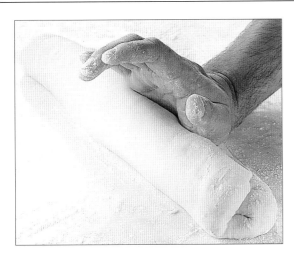

4 Gently press down with the palm of your hand along the seam to seal the fold. Place the dough seam side down. Press evenly with the palms of both hands and roll the dough backward and forward to achieve the desired length as specified in the recipe.

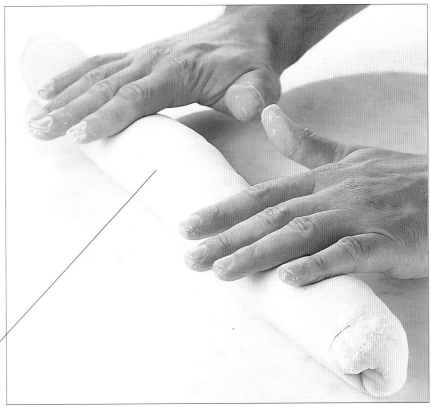

MAKING A BAGUETTE

TO MAKE A BAGUETTE, shape the dough as for a long loaf following steps 1–4. With hands placed at either end of the loaf, continue to gently roll the dough, backward and forward, moving both hands outward along the loaf. If the dough resists or tightens, allow it to rest for 5 minutes. Repeat the rolling action until an even thickness and the desired length are achieved.

Roll the dough while moving hands outward along the loaf

SHAPING DOUGH FOR A LOAF PAN

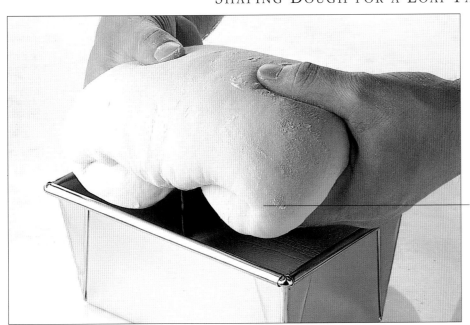

Shape the dough as for a long loaf up to step 3, opposite. Place the dough seam side down on the work surface. Use the straightened fingers of both hands to gently roll the dough backward and forward. Continue until the dough is the same length as the pan and is an even thickness. Lift the dough off the work surface. Tuck under the ends and place the dough into the prepared pan, seam side down.

Fold the dough to fit the length of the pan

SHAPING A ROUND LOAF

1 Gently press your fingers into the base of the rounded dough (*see page 51*) while holding it with both hands, as you would the steering wheel of a car. Rotate the dough between your cupped hands. As the dough is turned, exert light pressure with the tips of your fingers, while tucking the sides of the dough under what will become the base of the loaf.

2 When the dough becomes smooth and rounded, place the base of the loaf face down on a lightly floured work surface. Cup both hands around the dough and rotate it continuously in a steady, clockwise motion (*see Chafing, page 51*) until a smooth, evenly shaped round is formed. Turn the dough over so that the base is now facing upward and pinch the seam, or "key," together. Place the loaf "key" side down on a baking sheet.

SHAPING AN OVAL LOAF

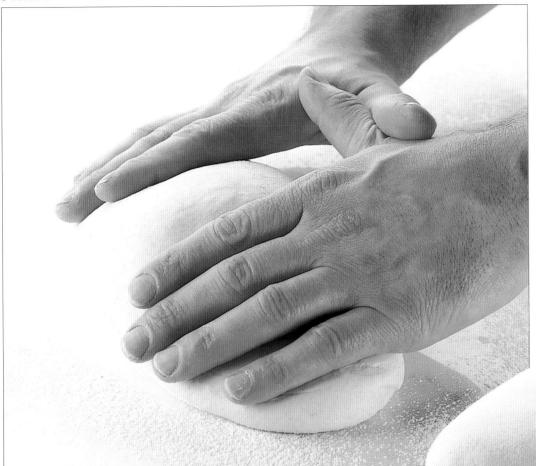

SHAPE THE DOUGH into a round loaf, following the directions given opposite. Place the palms of your hands on either side of the round and gently roll the dough backward and forward, keeping your hands in the same position. Continue to roll the dough until the ends become slightly tapered and the desired shape is achieved.

FINISHED SHAPE

ROUND ROLLS

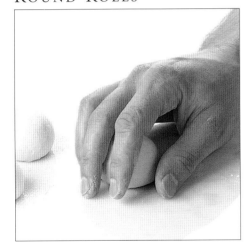

TO SHAPE ROUND ROLLS, divide the dough into pieces, each the size of a small lemon. Press down on the pieces to expel any air bubbles. Cup the palm of your hand over each piece and roll it over an unfloured surface until it forms a smooth ball.

KNOTTED ROLLS

TO SHAPE KNOTTED ROLLS, divide the dough into pieces, each the size of a small lemon. Use the palm of your hand to roll each piece on an unfloured surface to form a rope, 12 inches long and ½ inch thick. Tie each rope into a knot.

TWISTED ROLLS

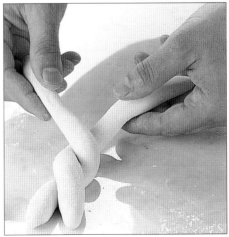

TO SHAPE TWISTED ROLLS, divide the dough into pieces, each the size of a small lemon. Use the palm of your hand to roll each piece on an unfloured surface to form a rope, 12 inches long and ½ inch thick. Twist two of the ropes around each other.

SHAPING A RING

1 Shape the dough into a round (*see page 54*), then flatten the top of the dough with the palm of your hand. Make a hole in the center of the dough: place the heel of your hand in the center of the dough and press down to the work surface.

Keep your fingers straightened and apply pressure evenly

2 Using both hands, lightly push out the dough with straightened fingers and run them around the inside edge of the hole. Apply pressure evenly to stretch the hole to 6 inches across.

FINISHED SHAPE

BRAIDING

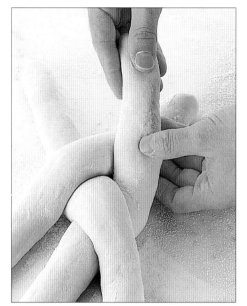
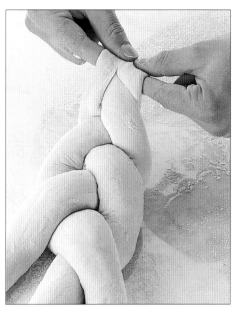
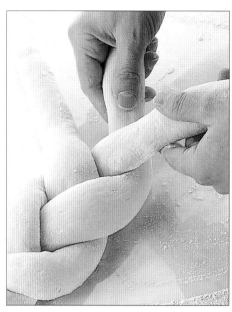

1 Divide the dough into three pieces and roll each one into a 16-inch-long rope. Line up the ropes at a right angle to the edge of the work surface. Start from the center of the ropes and braid toward yourself, working from left to right.

2 Continue braiding the ropes until you reach the end. Press the ends together with your fingers and tuck them neatly under the bottom of the braid. Turn the shaped dough around so that the unbraided end is now facing you.

3 Again, working from the center, braid the ropes from left to right until you reach the end. Press the ends together, tuck them neatly under the bottom of the braid to finish. Place the braid on a baking sheet.

PROOFING

PROOFING IS REFERRED TO as the final rise. Shaped dough is left to rise until doubled in size (unless otherwise specified in the recipe) on a prepared baking sheet or in a pan just before baking. Proofing is best done in a warm, draft-free place. In an exceptionally cold kitchen, a low oven or one heated with just the pilot light is a good option. Preheat the oven for baking halfway through the proofing time; remove the bread while the oven preheats.

Avoid overproofing by testing for doneness; press on the dough lightly with your fingertip. The shaped dough is ready to bake when it feels spongy rather than firm and the indentation made with your fingertip springs back slowly. It is best to put bread in the oven a little early (see page 162). Do not let shaped dough spread or deflate: overproofing can cause the dough to collapse when it is touched or slashed, or when it is placed in a hot oven.

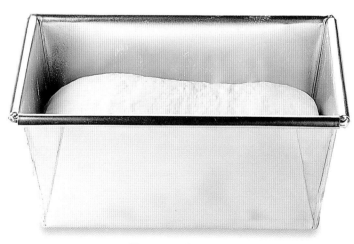

UNPROOFED DOUGH

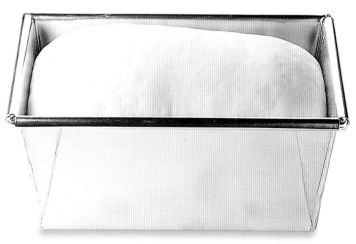

PROOFED DOUGH

GLAZING

DDING THE FINISHING TOUCHES to a bread is usually done after proofing. Glazes can affect the finished taste and texture of the crust as well as the appearance. A glaze is applied either before or after baking, depending on the glaze and the effect desired. Some glazes can be brushed on both before and after baking. When applying a glaze before baking, be careful not to "glue" the loaf to the rim of the loaf pan or the baking sheet. This not only will make it difficult to remove the loaf from the pan, but can prevent the loaf from expanding fully in the oven.

PREPARING AN EGG WASH

2 Use a clean, soft pastry brush to gently apply the egg wash to the shaped and proofed dough before baking. For an extra golden sheen, allow the first egg-wash coating to dry, then apply a second layer of glaze immediately before baking.

1 A basic egg wash will give a shiny, golden look to the crust. It can also be used as an "adhesive" to be applied before any of the toppings described on pages 60–61. To prepare, beat together 1 egg and 1 tablespoon of water or milk, and a pinch of salt.

Place the shaped dough on a baking sheet, prepared as directed by the recipe, before applying the glaze

Use a clean, soft pastry brush to apply the glaze

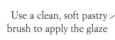

TYPES OF GLAZES – BEFORE AND AFTER BAKING

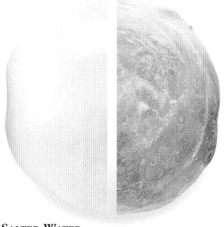

EGG WASH
For a shiny, golden-brown crust, brush the dough with the egg wash (see opposite) before baking.

MILK
For a golden crust, brush the dough with milk before baking. For a slightly sweeter glaze, dissolve a little sugar in warm milk.

SALTED WATER
For a light shine and a crisp baked crust, brush the dough with lightly salted water immediately before baking.

HONEY
For a soft, sweet, sticky crust, brush a baked, still-warm bread with honey. Alternatively, try molasses or corn syrup.

OLIVE OIL
For both added flavor and shine, brush the dough with olive oil immediately before and after baking.

CORNSTARCH
For a chewy crust, brush the dough with a mixture of cornstarch and water that has been cooked until translucent and then cooled.

SOY POWDER AND WATER
Make a vegan version of egg wash by using a mixture of soy powder and water.

GLAZING AFTER BAKING

Transfer the loaf or rolls to a wire cooling rack, then apply the prepared glaze using a soft pastry brush while the bread is still warm. Glazes are applied after baking to add flavor to the bread and to soften the texture of the crust.

TOPPING

Toppings offer many ways to finish a bread before baking. If a flavoring has been used to make the dough, then the loaf may be topped with the same ingredient, providing a clue to the hidden flavor inside. Toppings can also be used to complement a bread or simply to add a decorative touch. Toppings can be applied at different times: before proofing, the dough can be rolled in the topping; after proofing, the dough must be handled more gently by sprinkling the topping over the dough or using a strainer to create a light dusting.

METHODS OF TOPPING

BEFORE PROOFING

SPRINKLE SEEDS or other fine toppings onto a work surface. Gently press the shaped dough into the topping before placing it on a prepared baking sheet to proof.

AFTER PROOFING

SPRINKLE COARSE TOPPINGS like chopped nuts or grated cheese over the glazed dough (*see page 58*) after the proofing stage or immediately before baking.

BEFORE AND AFTER

USE A FINE MESH STRAINER to lightly dust the shaped dough with flour before and after proofing. This will give the crust a dusty, golden finish.

TYPES OF TOPPINGS – BEFORE AND AFTER BAKING

CRACKED WHEAT
For a crunchy crust, gently press the shaped dough into a bowl of cracked wheat before placing on a baking sheet to proof.

BRAN FLAKES
To add texture and fiber, glaze the shaped dough with an egg wash (see page 58) and sprinkle bran flakes over the top after proofing.

ROLLED OATS
To decorate, glaze the shaped dough with an egg wash (see page 58) and sprinkle with rolled oats after proofing.

WHITE FLOUR
To create a dusty, golden finish, sift a light dusting of flour over the shaped dough both before proofing and before baking.

GRANULATED SUGAR
For a sweet, crackly crust, glaze the shaped dough with an egg wash (see page 58) and sift sugar lightly over it after proofing.

PAPRIKA
For added spice and color, sprinkle the shaped dough with paprika or another ground spice after proofing.

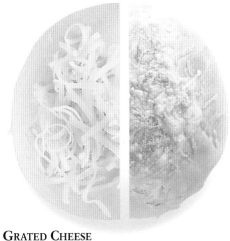

COARSE SALT
For a salty, crispy crust, glaze the shaped dough with an egg wash (see page 58) and sprinkle with coarse salt after proofing .

GRATED CHEESE
For a tangy and chewy crust, glaze the shaped dough with an egg wash (see page 58) and sprinkle with grated cheese after proofing.

FINE CORNMEAL
For color and a crisp texture, glaze the shaped dough with water only (see page 58) and sprinkle with fine cornmeal after proofing.

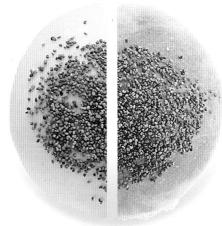

POPPY SEEDS
For a crunchy texture, glaze the shaped dough with an egg wash (see page 58) and sprinkle with poppy seeds after proofing.

PUMPKIN SEEDS
Arrange pumpkin seeds over the top for a flavorful decoration. Gently press them into the shaped dough before proofing.

FRESH HERBS
Use fresh herbs, such as rosemary and thyme, to add flavor and color. Press them into the shaped dough after proofing.

PREPARING FOR BAKING

SLASHING A LOAF before baking has both a functional and a decorative purpose. Cuts made through the surface of the dough allow the bread to rise and expand as it bakes without tearing or cracking along the sides or bottom. The deeper the slashes, the more the bread will open when baked, giving the baked loaf a maximum area of crust. It is best to cut the slashes using an extremely sharp blade and quick, firm strokes. If you hesitate as you slash, the dough will stick to the blade and tear. The use of steam in the oven before or during baking produces a moist heat that helps create a glazed, crisp crust on the loaf.

SLASHING THE LOAF

USING A BLADE

A RAZOR-SHARP BLADE is the best tool for making clean, perfect slashes. It is worth investing in a scalpel that allows you to safely hold the blade. Use decisive strokes to make the slashes clean and crisp. Keep the slashes equal in depth and length.

SLASHING A PAN LOAF

A LONG SLASH, about ½ inch deep, will allow a pan loaf to rise and open evenly when baked, without breaking open at the sides. With a firm, steady hand, plunge the blade into the surface of the dough and draw it quickly along the length of the loaf.

USING SCISSORS

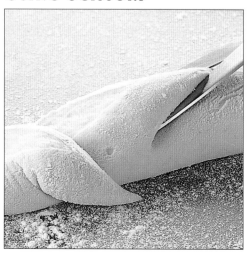

SHARP SCISSORS are a helpful and effective tool for making decorative slashes. Hold a pair of scissors almost horizontally to cut a *Baguette* into the *Pain d'Epi* variation. Cut about three-quarters of the way through the dough, leaving about 2 inches between each cut. Gently place the flaps to alternate sides.

QUICK SNIPS with a pair of sharp scissors produce a rough, sculptural cut. This is an effective alternative to using a scapel.

APPLYING STEAM TO THE OVEN

STEAM PLAYS AN IMPORTANT role in many bread recipes, especially those that require a crisp, crusty exterior. It is introduced into the oven before and sometimes during baking. The moisture in the air surrounding the bread in the oven affects both its texture and its appearance. Moisture helps soften the crust during the initial stages of baking. This allows the dough to rise fully and a thin, crisp crust to form. Moisture also helps caramelize the natural sugars in the bread, resulting in a rich, golden brown crust.

USING A SPRAYER

APPLY STEAM WITH A WATER SPRAYER after placing the loaf in the preheated oven. Mist the oven walls eight to ten times, then repeat the process after 2 minutes and again after 2 minutes more. Shut the door rapidly each time to minimize any heat loss from the oven. Be careful to spray only the sides of the oven, avoiding the oven light, electric heating coils, and oven fan.

USING ICE CUBES

APPLY STEAM BY PLACING A WIDE DISH filled with ice cubes on the bottom rack or floor of the oven while the oven preheats. Place the loaf in the oven before the ice cubes have completely melted. When the ice cubes have melted, carefully remove the dish from the oven. This should occur within the first 15–20 minutes of the bread's baking time.

USING CERAMIC TILES

LINE THE BOTTOM RACK of the oven with unglazed ceramic tiles, leaving 2 inches of air space all the way around the tiles and the oven wall to allow for air circulation. The tiles will produce a steady, radiating heat as well as help retain a maximum amount of moisture in the oven. When tiles are used in combination with the applied steam methods shown, and the bread is baked directly on the tiled surface, it will form the crispest crust of the three methods.

BAKING

BAKING IS THE CULMINATION of the breadmaking process when all your hard work and patience are rewarded. For a successful finished loaf, follow these simple guidelines: use a good thermometer to regulate the temperature of the oven; preheat to the correct temperature before placing the bread in the oven to bake; be sure of the exact baking time before beginning; and always use a kitchen timer to keep track of the time. An important key to proficient baking lies in knowing your oven and being able to control its temperature closely—each one is slightly different and has its own peculiarities.

BAKING STAGES

1 When the bread is placed in the hot oven, the heat turns the moisture in the dough to steam, causing the loaf to rise rapidly in the first 20 minutes of baking. The heat then penetrates the bread, killing the active yeast cells and allowing the exterior crust to form.

GETTING TO KNOW YOUR OVEN
Since each oven is different, it is difficult to establish hard-and-fast rules for breadmaking, such as oven shelf position. The only solution is increased familiarity with your oven. Using an oven thermometer before and during baking allows you to observe any variations in temperature and to make adjustments. If you find you have "hot spots" (uneven heat) in your oven, it is important to turn the bread halfway through baking.

2 As the exterior crust forms, the natural sugars in the dough caramelize, creating a golden color. The baking time is specified in each recipe. High humidity, however, can sometimes extend the required baking time and must be taken into consideration on the day of baking.

The dough's natural sugars caramelize to give a golden crust

TESTING FOR DONENESS

UNDERCOOKING BREAD IS A common mistake of the novice baker. Bread is indigestible when it has been undercooked, so it is important to test for doneness. A well-baked bread should be golden brown, not too pale or too dark in color. The texture and feel of the bread should be firm to the touch without seeming hard. The best test, however, is to listen to the sound of the baked loaf when it is tapped on the underside. It should sound slightly hollow when it has been properly cooked.

COOLING

IT IS IMPORTANT TO ALLOW a freshly baked loaf to cool on a wire rack. As the loaf cools, steam from the middle works its way toward the crust, causing it to soften. Cooling baked bread on a wire rack prevents the bottom crust from becoming damp and soggy.

SLICING

WHEN SLICING BREAD, use a sharp, serrated bread knife and a clean bread board. Bread should be left to cool slightly before slicing. Use a steady, sawing motion across the top of the bread to prevent the weight of the knife from crushing the loaf or tearing the crust.

USING A BREAD MACHINE

THE MANUFACTURER'S INSTRUCTION MANUAL is an invaluable resource for getting the best results from your machine. A bread machine will mix, knead, rise, and bake the loaf, yet machine models vary in the shape and size of loaf they make as well as the way they operate. Some machines have programmable cycles for making different kinds of bread dough; others offer fewer alternatives. A recipe booklet comes with most models. Master a few of these recipes to familiarize yourself with the way your machine works, its possibilities and its limitations. Use the experience to adapt the recipes in this book following the general guidelines given below.

1 Add the ingredients to the baking cylinder in the order suggested by the instruction manual. This will vary, depending on the machine model you have. The manufacturer's instructions will tell you what type of yeast to use. Best results are achieved with a yeast made for bread machines, although instant yeast also works. Place the baking cylinder inside the machine, select the setting on the control panel, according to the manual, and press start.

HANDY TIPS

• *Pay attention to the order in which the ingredients are added to the machine—it does make a difference.*

• *Keep the lid open to watch the mixing and kneading cycles, but make sure the lid is shut during rising and baking.*

• *Use the handle of a wooden spoon to remove the kneading paddle from the bottom of the hot finished loaf.*

2 Check the dough about 10 minutes into the kneading cycle. It should be smooth and soft at this stage (*right*). If it is too soft, add more flour 1 tablespoon at a time. If it is stiff, add more water 1 tablespoon at a time. Ingredients like nuts and dried fruit should be added in the last few minutes of the kneading cycle.

3 When the bread is baked, remove it immediately from the machine and the baking cylinder to prevent a soggy crust. Let it cool on a wire rack.

USING RECIPES FROM THIS BOOK

Depending on the capacity of your bread machine, many of the basic bread recipes, excluding those using a starter (*see pages 84–93*), may be mixed and kneaded by your bread machine. Most bread machines use instant yeast, which means eliminating the sponge method from the recipe instructions. Add the ingredients in the order suggested by the manufacturer's manual, and select the correct machine settings. Remove the dough from the machine after the rising period and before the proofing (final rise) and baking cycles begin. Instead, shape, proof, and bake according to the recipe.

STORING & FREEZING

SOME BREADS ARE BEST EATEN on the day of baking, but most home-baked breads will keep from several days up to a week. As a general rule, storage time depends on the ingredients used and the size of the loaf. A large, thick loaf will usually dry out more slowly than a small, thin one. Breads enriched with oil, butter, or eggs (*see pages 110–125*) tend to last longer than plain breads, and those made with a starter (*see pages 84–93*) also have a longer shelf life. Bread dough can easily be frozen, either before or after rising, which allows greater flexibility in the breadmaking schedule. Baked bread also freezes and defrosts successfully.

STORING BAKED BREAD

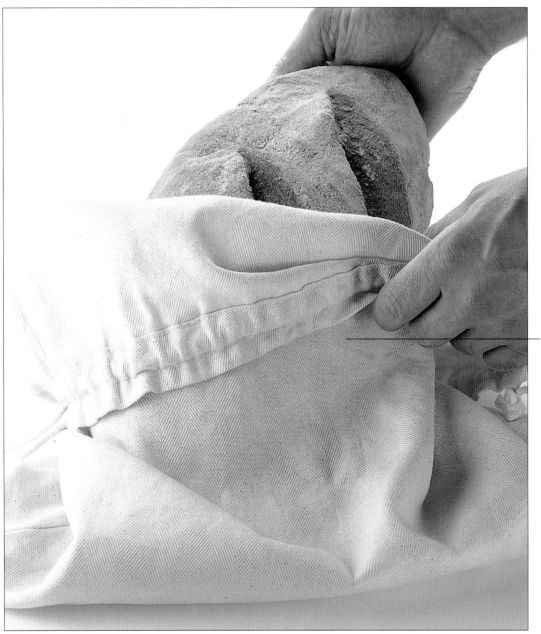

A clean, dry cloth bag is the best place to store bread after it has cooled

STORE BREAD only after it has cooled. Any residual warmth left in the bread will continue to give off steam, which will condense inside the wrapping or container and cause a stale texture and rapid molding. When the bread has completely cooled, wrap in a clean dry cloth or bread bag and store at room temperature. If stored like this, bread will remain fresh for 3–4 days. Never refrigerate bread; it dehydrates the bread and accelerates staling.

FRESHENING STALE BREAD

Spray the bread lightly with tap water, wrap in foil, and warm in an oven, 400°F, for 10 minutes. Microwave ovens are not recommended for freshening stale bread; microwaving tends to dry out and harden bread.

FREEZING UNRISEN DOUGH

FREEZING SHAPED DOUGH

WHEN AVAILABLE TIME IS LIMITED, dough can be frozen before rising and shaping. Mix and knead the dough as directed in the recipe. Brush the inside of a plastic freezer bag with oil and place the unrisen dough inside. Expel any air, leaving just enough space for the dough to rise slightly as it freezes. To thaw, place the dough in the refrigerator for 12–24 hours, until it has doubled in size. Remove from the refrigerator and bring the dough to room temperature. Shape, proof, and bake as directed.

WHEN IT IS MORE CONVENIENT, the dough can be frozen after shaping. Place the shaped dough on a baking sheet and cover tightly with plastic wrap. Then place the baking sheet in the freezer and leave just until the dough becomes firm. Store the dough in a plastic freezer bag. To thaw, remove the dough from the bag and place it in the refrigerator for 12–24 hours, until it has doubled in size. Remove from the refrigerator and leave at room temperature for 20 minutes. Bake as directed.

FREEZING BAKED BREAD

FRESHLY BAKED BREAD can be frozen successfully after it has completely cooled. Wrap the bread in heavy-duty foil, then place it in a plastic freezer bag; expel all the air before sealing. The bread will keep for up to 3 months.

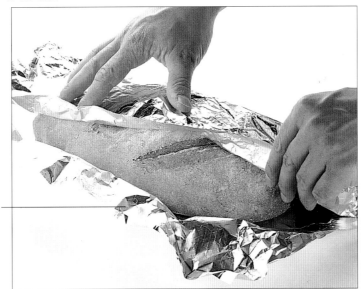

Use heavy-duty foil to wrap bread before freezing

DEFROSTING BREAD

Defrost bread slowly at a cool room temperature for 3–6 hours, or in the refrigerator for 8–10 hours. Bread that is defrosted slowly will retain its freshness for longer. Defrost bread in its wrapping to prevent it from drying out. For breads with a thick crust, crisp them in a low oven before serving. To defrost bread more quickly, place the wrapped loaf in a preheated oven, 400°F, for 45 minutes.

RECIPES

MORE THAN 100 BREADS CAN BE CREATED USING THIS RECIPE SECTION. EACH ONE IS A VARIATION ON A VERY SIMPLE THEME: FLOUR, WATER, LEAVEN, AND TIME. BEGIN WITH THE BASIC AND STARTER BREAD RECIPES, WHICH UTILIZE METHODS ILLUSTRATED IN THE BASIC TECHNIQUES. FLAVORED BREADS PROVIDE AN EXTRA TASTE DIMENSION, WHILE ENRICHED BREADS TRANSFORM BASIC BREAD DOUGH WITH THE ADDITION OF OIL, BUTTER, AND EGGS. QUICK, FLAT, AND FESTIVE BREADS OFFER OTHER DELICIOUS POSSIBILITIES FROM AROUND THE WORLD.

  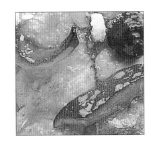

BASIC BREADS

THE RECIPES IN THIS SECTION require no advanced skills, only your hands, your attention, and your time. They represent the backbone of the book, by utilizing the skills covered in the Basic Techniques section. Read this section (*see pages 38–69*) first, and you will be able to tackle all the basic bread recipes with ease and confidence. These simple breads give the novice baker the opportunity to experiment, observe the transformation of the ingredients into bread, and gain valuable experience. Later on in the recipe section, other elements—such as starters, flavorings, and enrichments—are added to the basic ingredients of flour, water, and yeast. These additions introduce the baker to new techniques and skills illustrated with the recipes.

PAIN ORDINAIRE
PLAIN OR BASIC WHITE BREAD

Treat this recipe as a blueprint for the basic method of breadmaking. A wide variety of breads can be created using this simple dough recipe. For a more rustic flavor, substitute ⅓ cup of whole-wheat, rye, or barley flour for the same amount of unbleached flour. For an extra tender crumb, replace ¾ cup of the water with the same amount of yogurt or buttermilk and use it to add to the well in step 3.

INGREDIENTS

2 tsp dry yeast
1½ cups water
3¾ cups bread flour, sifted
1½ tsp salt

1 Sprinkle the yeast into ½ cup of the water in a bowl. Let stand for 5 minutes; stir to dissolve. Mix the flour and salt in a large bowl. Make a well in the center and pour in the dissolved yeast.

2 Use a wooden spoon to draw enough of the flour into the dissolved yeast to form a soft paste. Cover the bowl with a dish towel and let the paste "sponge" until frothy, loose, and slightly expanded, about 20 minutes.

3 Pour about half of the remaining water into the center of the well. Mix in the flour from the sides of the well. Stir in the reserved water, as needed, to form a firm, moist dough.

4 Turn the dough out onto a lightly floured work surface. Knead until smooth, shiny, and elastic, about 10 minutes.

5 Put the dough in a clean bowl and cover with a dish towel. Let rise until doubled in size, about 1½–2 hours. Punch down, then let rest for 10 minutes.

6 Shape the dough into a long loaf (*see pages 52–53*), about 14 inches in length. Place the shaped loaf on a floured baking sheet and cover with a dish towel. Proof until doubled in size, about 45 minutes.

7 Cut five diagonal slashes, each about ¼ inch deep, across the top of the loaf (*see page 62*). Bake in the preheated oven for 45 minutes, until golden and hollow sounding when tapped underneath. Cool on a wire rack.

To begin
Sponge method
Time: 20 minutes
(*see page 44*)

Rising
1½–2 hours
(*see pages 50–51*)

Proofing
45 minutes
(*see page 57*)

Oven temperature
425°F

Baking
45 minutes
Steam optional
(*see page 63*)

Yield
1 loaf

Yeast alternative
1 cake (0.6oz) yeast
(*see page 41*)

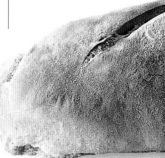
CLASSIC PAIN ORDINAIRE

SHAPING A COTTAGE LOAF

Divide the dough into ⅔ and ⅓. Shape each piece into a round loaf (see pages 54–55). Place the small loaf on top of the large loaf. Plunge two fingers into the centers of the stacked loaves to join them together.

VARIATIONS

Cottage Loaf

• Make one quantity Pain Ordinaire dough up to step 6.
• Shape the bread dough according to the instructions (*see left*).
• Place on a floured baking sheet and cover with a dish towel. Proof until doubled in size, about 45 minutes. Preheat the oven to 425°F.
• Sift a light dusting of flour on the top. Bake as directed in step 7.

Petits Pains (Bread Rolls)

• Make one quantity Pain Ordinaire dough up to step 6.
• Divide the bread dough into eight pieces and shape into smooth, round rolls (*see page 55*).
• Place on a floured baking sheet and cover with a dish towel. Proof until doubled in size, about 30 minutes. Preheat the oven to 425°F.
• Sift a dusting of flour on the top. Use a pair of scissors to snip an "X" in the center of each roll (*see page 62*).
• Bake for 25 minutes, until hollow sounding when tapped underneath. Cool on a wire rack.

Granary Pan Loaf

• Make one quantity Pain Ordinaire dough up to step 6, replacing the bread flour with the same amount of granary flour (*see page 29*) in step 1.
• Grease an 8 x 4 x 2½-inch loaf pan with oil. Shape the dough for a loaf pan (*see page 53*) and place the dough in the pan, seam side down.
• Cover with a dish towel and proof until the dough is ½ inch below the top of the pan, about 30 minutes.
• If desired, cut a lengthwise slash (*see page 62*) for a split pan loaf. Let the dough rise further until it is ½ inch above the top of the pan. Preheat the oven to 425°F.
• Brush the top with water and bake in the preheated oven for 20 minutes. Reduce the oven to 400°F and bake for 15–20 minutes, until hollow sounding when tapped. Turn out onto a wire rack to cool.

— HANDY TIPS —

• *Use lukewarm water to dissolve the yeast (see page 41). Lukewarm water should be comfortable to the touch, not too hot, but not too cool.*

• *It is important that the dough is soft and not too dry before it is kneaded. Add more water 1 tablespoon at a time, as needed, to achieve the consistency indicated in the recipe.*

• *When kneading the dough, use extra flour sparingly. Work the dough slowly and firmly; it will gradually become more elastic and easier to knead.*

COTTAGE LOAF

GRANARY PAN LOAF

PETITS PAINS

COUNTRY OATMEAL BREAD

Sometimes called monastery bread, this coarse, crunchy British bread originated in northern England. It is often eaten for breakfast or an afternoon snack, thickly spread with yellow, salted butter and fragrant honey, or with a chunk of cheddar cheese and a glass of beer.

INGREDIENTS

2 tsp dry yeast

1½ cups water

2 cups whole-wheat flour

1 cup bread flour

1½ cups medium oatmeal

1½ tsp salt

1 tsp honey

rolled oats, for topping

1 Sprinkle the yeast into ½ cup of the water in a bowl. Let stand for 5 minutes; stir to dissolve. Mix the flours, oatmeal, and salt in a large bowl. Make a well in the center and pour in the dissolved yeast and the honey.

2 Pour about half of the remaining water into the well. Mix in the flour, then stir in the reserved water, as needed, to form a stiff, sticky dough.

3 Turn the dough out onto a work surface lightly sprinkled with oatmeal. Knead until smooth and elastic, about 10 minutes.

4 Put the dough in a bowl and cover with a dish towel. Let rise until doubled in size, about 1½–2 hours. Punch down, then let rest for 10 minutes. Grease an 8 x 4 x 2½-inch loaf pan.

5 Shape the dough for a loaf pan (*see page 53*). Place the dough in the pan, seam side down. Cover with a dish towel and proof until doubled in size, about 1 hour.

6 Brush the loaf lightly with water and sprinkle the rolled oats over the top. Bake in the preheated oven for 1 hour, until golden brown and hollow sounding when tapped underneath. Turn out onto a wire rack to cool.

VARIATIONS

Barley Bread

• Make one quantity Country Oatmeal Bread dough up to step 6, replacing the flours with 2 cups bread flour, ¾ cup barley flour, and 1 cup whole-wheat flour. Preheat the oven to 400°F.

• Brush the loaf lightly with water and sprinkle with barley flakes.

• Bake in the preheated oven for 1 hour, until golden brown and hollow sounding when tapped underneath. Turn out onto a wire rack to cool.

Oatmeal Rolls

• Make one quantity Country Oatmeal Bread dough up to step 5.

• Divide the dough into 16 equal pieces and shape into smooth, round rolls (*see page 55*). Place the rolls on two greased baking sheets. Cover with a dish towel and proof until doubled in size, about 30–45 minutes. Preheat the oven to 400°F.

• Brush the rolls with water and sprinkle with rolled oats.

• Bake in the preheated oven for 20–30 minutes, until golden and hollow sounding when tapped underneath. Cool on a wire rack.

 Rising
1½–2 hours
(*see pages 50–51*)

 Proofing
1 hour
(*see page 57*)

 Oven temperature
400°F

 Baking
1 hour
Steam optional
(*see page 63*)

 Yield
1 loaf

 Yeast alternative
1 cake (0.6oz) yeast
(*see page 41*)

DAKTYLA
GREEK VILLAGE BREAD

This sesame seed-coated bread is traditionally made with "yellow" or "country" flour, a blend of white and whole-wheat flour mixed with finely ground cornmeal. Alternatively, it can be made with just bread flour. In Greece, the bread is commonly known as Daktyla, *meaning "fingers," because it is broken into fingers of bread to eat.*

INGREDIENTS

2 tsp dry yeast
1¼ cups water
2½ cups bread flour
⅔ cup whole-wheat flour
½ cup fine cornmeal
1 tsp salt
1 tbsp olive oil
1 tbsp honey
1 tbsp milk, plus extra to glaze
sesame seeds, to decorate

1 Sprinkle the yeast into ½ cup of the water in a bowl. Let sit for 5 minutes; stir to dissolve. Mix the flours, cornmeal, and salt thoroughly in a large bowl. Make a well in t he center and pour in the dissolved yeast.

2 Use a wooden spoon to draw enough of the flour into the dissolved yeast to form a soft paste. Cover the bowl with a dish towel and let "sponge" until frothy and risen, 20 minutes. Add the oil, honey, and milk to the sponge.

3 Pour about half of the remaining water into the well. Mix in the flour. Stir in the reserved water, as needed, to form a firm, moist dough.

4 Turn the dough out onto a lightly floured work surface. Knead until smooth, shiny, and elastic, about 10 minutes.

5 Put the dough in a clean bowl and cover with a dish towel. Let rise until doubled in size, about 1½ hours. Punch down, then let rest for 10 minutes.

6 Divide the dough into six equal pieces. Shape each piece into an oblong; arrange them in a row, just touching, on a floured baking sheet. Cover with a dish towel and proof until doubled in size, about 1 hour.

7 Brush the top of the loaf with milk and sprinkle with the sesame seeds. Bake in the preheated oven for 45 minutes, until hollow sounding when tapped underneath. Cool on a wire rack.

To begin
Sponge method
Time: 20 minutes
(*see page 44*)

Rising
1½ hours
(*see pages 50–51*)

Proofing
1 hour
(*see page 57*)

Oven temperature
425°F

Baking
45 minutes
Steam optional
(*see page 63*)

Yield
1 loaf

Yeast alternative
1 cake (0.6oz) yeast
(*see page 41*)

VICTORIAN MILK BREAD

This is a bread with a soft crust and crumb that keeps well and makes crisp, nutty toast. The elegant, S-shaped loaf is easy to make. This is also a very good dough for making a decorative braid (see page 57).

INGREDIENTS

2 tsp dry yeast

1 tsp sugar

1½ cups lukewarm milk

3¼ cups bread flour

1½ tsp salt

egg glaze, made with 1 egg and 1 tbsp milk (see page 58)

1 Sprinkle the yeast and sugar into ½ cup of milk in a bowl. Let stand for 5 minutes; stir to dissolve. Stir in half of the remaining milk.

2 Mix the flour and salt in a large bowl. Make a well in the center and pour in the dissolved yeast. Mix in the flour. Stir in the reserved milk to form a sticky dough.

3 Turn the dough out onto a lightly floured work surface. Knead the dough until smooth and elastic, about 10 minutes.

4 Put the dough in a clean bowl and cover with a dish towel. Let rise for 45 minutes. Punch down, cover, and let the dough rise again until doubled in size, about 45 minutes.

5 Grease an 8 x 4 x 2½-inch loaf pan. Shape the dough into an S-shape (*see right*). Cover with a dish towel. Proof until the dough is 1 inch above the top of the pan, about 1 hour.

6 Brush the top of the loaf with the egg glaze. Bake in the preheated oven for 45 minutes, until golden and hollow sounding when tapped underneath. Turn out onto a wire rack to cool.

VARIATION
Bloomer
(see page 16 for illustration)

• Make one quantity Victorian Milk Bread dough, replacing half the milk with water, up to step 4.

• Let rise for 2 hours. Punch down and let rest for 5 minutes.

• Shape into a long loaf, about 10 inches in length and 5 inches wide (*see pages 52–53*). Proof as directed, about 1 hour.

• Cut five deep slashes (*see page 62*) across the top of the loaf. Preheat the oven to 425°F.

• Sift a fine layer of flour on the top. Bake as directed in step 6.

 Rising
1½ hours
(see pages 50–51)

 Proofing
1 hour
(see page 57)

 Oven temperature
400°F

 Baking
45 minutes

 Yield
1 loaf

 Yeast alternative
1 cake (0.6oz) yeast
(see page 41)

SHAPING THE DOUGH

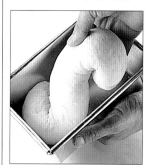

Shape the dough into a long loaf (see pages 52–53), about 16 inches in length and 3¼ inches wide. Turn the shaped dough over at each end to form an S-shape. Place the shaped dough in the greased loaf pan. Continue as directed in step 5.

SCOTS BAPS

Scots Baps are best eaten warm straight from the oven. They are a special treat at breakfast when filled with grilled bacon and a fried egg. The mixture of milk and water gives the rolls a tender crumb, and the extra dusting of flour gives them a soft crust.

INGREDIENTS

¼ cup lukewarm milk

¼ cup water

2 tsp dry yeast

1 tsp sugar

3¾ cups bread flour

1½ tsp salt

1 tbsp milk, to glaze

1 Combine the milk and water in a liquid measuring cup. Sprinkle the yeast and sugar into ½ cup of the milk and water mixture in a separate bowl. Let stand for 5 minutes; stir to dissolve. Stir in half of the remaining milk and water mixture.

2 Mix the flour and salt in a large bowl. Make a well in the center and pour in the dissolved yeast. Mix in the flour. Stir in the reserved milk and water, as needed, to form a sticky dough.

3 Turn the dough out onto a lightly floured work surface. Knead the dough until smooth and elastic, about 10 minutes.

4 Put the dough in a clean bowl and cover with a dish towel. Let rise until doubled in size, about 1 hour. Punch down, then let rest for 10 minutes.

5 Divide the dough into eight equal pieces. Shape each piece of dough into a flat oval, about ½ inch thick. Place on a floured baking sheet. Brush each bap with milk and sift a heavy dusting of flour over each.

6 Proof, uncovered, until doubled in size, 30–45 minutes.

7 Sift a heavy dusting of flour over each bap. Use your thumb to make an impression in the center of each bap, about ½ inch deep.

8 Bake in the preheated oven for 15–20 minutes, until risen and golden. Cover with a dish towel for 10 minutes and cool on a wire rack.

VARIATION
Kentish Huffkins

• Make one quantity Scots Baps dough up to step 4.

• Divide the dough into 12 equal pieces. Shape each piece of dough into smooth ball (*see page 55*). Place on a floured baking sheet.

• Use a floured finger to form a deep indentation in the center of each roll. Proof until doubled in size, 30–45 minutes. Preheat the oven to 400°F.

• Bake as directed in step 8. Cool on a wire rack. Fill the indentation with jam and thick cream to serve.

 Rising
1 hour
(*see pages 50–51*)

 Proofing
30–45 minutes
(*see page 57*)

 Oven temperature
400°F

 Baking
15–20 minutes

 Yield
8 baps

 Yeast alternative
1 cake (0.6oz) yeast
(*see page 41*)

BALLYMALOE BROWN BREAD

This no-knead, one-rise bread was introduced by Doris Grant in her book Your Daily Bread. *This recipe is an improved version devised by Myrtle Allen, founder of the now legendary Ballymaloe House hotel and cooking school in County Cork, Ireland.*

INGREDIENTS

3½ tsp dry yeast

1⅔ cups water

1 tsp molasses

3¾ cups whole-wheat flour

2 tsp salt

1 Grease an 8 x 4 x 2½-inch loaf pan and warm it in a preheated oven, 250°F, for 10 minutes.

2 Sprinkle the yeast into ⅔ cup of the water in a bowl. Let stand for 5 minutes; stir to dissolve. Add the molasses. Let stand for 10 minutes, until frothy. Add the remaining water and stir.

3 Mix the flour and salt in a large bowl. Make a well in the center and pour in the dissolved yeast. Stir in the flour to form a thick batter.

4 Use your hands to mix the batter gently in the bowl for 1 minute, until it begins to leave the sides of the bowl clean and forms a soft, sticky dough.

5 Place the dough in the prepared pan and cover with a dish towel. Proof until the dough is ½ inch above the top of the pan, about 25–30 minutes.

6 Bake in the preheated oven at 425°F for 30 minutes, then lower the oven to 400°F and bake for 15 minutes.

7 Turn the loaf out of the pan and onto a baking sheet. Return the bread, bottom side up, to the oven. Bake 10 minutes more, until golden and hollow sounding when tapped underneath. Let cool on a wire rack.

 Proofing
25–30 minutes
(*see page 57*)

 Oven temperature
425°F

 Baking
55 minutes

 Yield
1 loaf

 Yeast alternative
1¾ cakes
(0.6oz-sized) yeast
(*see page 41*)

BROA

PORTUGUESE CORN BREAD

This yellow bread originated in the province of Beira Alta in northern Portugal, but is now found countrywide. The proportion of wheat to cornmeal varies from bakery to bakery and region to region. Broa is a traditional accompaniment to caldo verde, *the northern region's famous kale and sausage soup. (See page 19 for an illustration of the bread.)*

INGREDIENTS

2 tsp dry yeast

½ cup plus 2 tbsp lukewarm milk

¾ cup water

1¼ cup yellow cornmeal

2¼ cups bread flour, sifted

1½ tsp salt

1 tbsp olive oil

1 Sprinkle the yeast into the milk in a bowl. Let stand for 5 minutes; stir with a wooden spoon. Add the water to the milk. Mix the cornmeal, flour, and salt in a large bowl. Make a well in the center and pour in the dissolved yeast and olive oil.

2 Mix in the flour to form a firm and moist, but not sticky dough that leaves the sides of the bowl.

3 Turn the dough out onto a lightly floured work surface. Knead the dough until smooth and elastic, about 10 minutes.

4 Put the dough in a clean bowl and cover with a dish towel. Let rise until doubled in size, about 1½ hours. Punch down, then let rest for 10 minutes.

5 Shape into a round loaf (*see page 54*). Place on a baking sheet sprinkled with cornmeal and cover with a dish towel. Proof until doubled in size, about 1 hour.

6 Dust the loaf with cornmeal. Bake in the preheated oven for 45 minutes, until golden and hollow sounding when tapped underneath. Cool on a wire rack.

 Rising
1½ hours
(*see pages 50–51*)

 Proofing
1 hour
(*see page 57*)

 Oven temperature
400°F

 Baking
45 minutes
Steam optional
(*see page 63*)

 Yield
1 loaf

 Yeast alternative
1 cake (0.6oz) yeast
(*see page 41*)

BAGUETTE
FRENCH STICK

The name of this long, thin loaf with a crisp, golden crust and light, chewy interior translates literally to "little rod" and, in French, also means a fairy's wand or a conductor's baton. The French say that it is always best to buy two Baguettes because one is always half eaten by the time it arrives home.

BAGUETTE

INGREDIENTS
2½ tsp dry yeast

1¼ cups water

3¼ cups bread flour

1½ tsp salt

1 Sprinkle the yeast into 1¼ cups of the water in a bowl. Let stand for 5 minutes; stir to dissolve. Mix the flour and salt in a large bowl. Make a well in the center and pour in the dissolved yeast.

2 Use a wooden spoon to draw enough of the flour into the dissolved yeast to form a soft paste. Cover the bowl with a dish towel and let "sponge" until frothy and risen, 20 minutes.

3 Mix in the flour and add the remaining water, as needed, 1 tablespoon at a time, to form a soft, sticky dough.

4 Turn out onto a lightly floured work surface. Knead until soft, smooth, and supple, about 10 minutes. Try to avoid adding extra flour while kneading the dough.

5 Put the dough in a clean bowl and cover with a dish towel. Let rise until doubled in size, about 1½ hours.

6 Punch down, re-cover, and let rise for 45 minutes longer. Punch down again, re-cover, and let rise until doubled in size, about 45 minutes.

7 Divide the dough into two equal pieces and shape into two baguettes (*see pages 52–53*), each about 12 inches in length. Place on a floured baking sheet or in a floured baguette tray (*see page 37*); cover with a dish towel. Proof until doubled in size, about 50 minutes.

8 Cut several diagonal slashes (*see page 62*) across the top. Bake in the preheated oven for 20–25 minutes, until golden and hollow sounding when tapped underneath. Cool on a wire rack.

VARIATIONS
Pistolets (Split Rolls)
(see page 12 for illustration)
• Make one quantity Baguette dough up to step 7. Divide the dough into eight equal pieces and shape each piece into a smooth ball (*see page 55*).
• Sift a dusting of flour over the dough balls. Use the handle of a wooden spoon to make a deep indentation across the center of each ball, pressing down through the dough almost to the work surface. Place the split rolls well apart on a floured baking sheet.
• Sift a dusting of flour over each roll to prevent the two halves of the roll from sticking together during proofing and baking.
• Cover with a dish towel and proof until doubled in size, about 30 minutes. Preheat the oven to 425°F.
• Bake as directed in step 8. Cool on a wire rack.
• This roll shape also works well when made with Pain Ordinaire dough (*see page 72*) and Pain de Campagne dough (*see page 84*).

Pain d'Epi ("Ear of Wheat")
• Make one quantity Baguette dough up to step 7. Divide the dough and shape into two baguettes (*see pages 52–53*) about 12 inches long. Use sharp scissors to cut the loaves, as directed on page 62.
• Place on a floured baking sheet; cover with a dish towel. Proof until doubled in size, about 50 minutes. Preheat the oven to 425°F. Bake as directed in step 8. Cool on a wire rack.

To begin
Sponge method
Time: 20 minutes
(*see page 44*)

Rising
3 hours
(*see pages 50–51*)

Proofing
50 minutes
(*see page 57*)

Oven temperature
475°F

Baking
20–25 minutes
Steam optional
(*see page 63*)

Yield
2 loaves

Yeast alternative
1¼ cakes
(0.6oz-sized) yeast
(*see page 41*)

PAIN D'EPI

GRISSINI TORINESI
ITALIAN BREADSTICKS

These famous Italian breadsticks are served with an antipasto or an appetizer. They are easily digested, designed not to curb the diner's appetite for the rest of the meal. Coat them with any spice, herb, or seed you desire: replace the sesame seeds with the topping of your choice, such as coarse sea salt, fresh rosemary, or dried fennel seeds. For more topping ideas, see pages 60–61. Sprinkle the topping over the sticks after they have been brushed with the egg glaze and bake as directed in step 6.

INGREDIENTS

2 tsp dry yeast
1 cup plus 2 tbsp water
1 tsp malt extract
3¼ cups bread flour, sifted
2 tsp salt
3 tbsp olive oil
2 tbsp semolina
egg glaze, made with 1 egg yolk and 1 tbsp water (see page 58)
sesame seeds, for topping

1 Sprinkle the yeast into ½ cup of the water in a bowl. Let stand for 5 minutes, then add the malt extract; stir to dissolve. Mix the flour and the salt in a large bowl. Make a well in the center and pour in the dissolved yeast and the olive oil.

2 Use a wooden spoon to draw in the flour from the sides. Stir in the remaining water, as needed, to form a firm, sticky dough.

3 Turn the dough out onto a well-floured work surface. Knead the dough until smooth and elastic, about 10 minutes. Cover with a dish towel and let rest for 10 minutes. Knead the dough for 10 minutes more.

4 Shape the dough into an 8 x 12-inch rectangle, ¾ inch thick. Cover with a dish towel; let rest for 10 minutes.

5 Lightly oil two baking sheets and sprinkle them with semolina. Cut the dough lengthwise into four equal pieces, then cut each piece lengthwise into ten strips. Stretch each strip until it is 10 inches long. Place the strips, about ½ inch apart, on the baking sheets.

6 Brush the strips with the egg glaze and sprinkle with sesame seeds. Bake in the preheated oven for 15–20 minutes. Transfer the sticks onto a wire rack, then let cool.

VARIATION
Picos (Spanish Bread Loops)
• Make one quantity Grissini Torinesi dough up to step 4.
• Divide the dough into two equal pieces. Shape each piece into a rectangle, about 6 x 8 inches. Cover with a dish towel, then let rest for 10 minutes. Preheat the oven to 425°F.
• Cut each rectangle lengthwise into 16 equal strips, then cut each dough strip in half to make 64 pieces of dough. Tie each strip in a single knot (see page 55). Place each knot on a lightly oiled baking sheet. Brush with water and, if desired, sprinkle with coarse sea salt.
• Bake as directed in step 6. Cool on a wire rack.

Oven temperature
400°F

Baking
15–20 minutes
Steam optional
(*see page 63*)

Yield
40 breadsticks

Yeast alternative
1 cake (0.6oz) yeast
(*see page 41*)

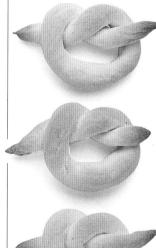
PICOS

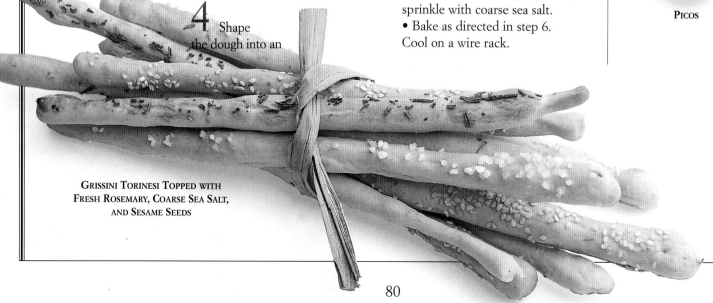
GRISSINI TORINESI TOPPED WITH FRESH ROSEMARY, COARSE SEA SALT, AND SESAME SEEDS

BAGELS

These chewy, ring-shaped white rolls were once the everyday bread of Eastern European Jews, but have since become equally associated with New York City and the classic breakfast of bagels and cream cheese. Before baking, the bagels are poached; this gives them their characteristically shiny, chewy exterior and dense, tender interior.

INGREDIENTS

2 tsp dry yeast

1½ tbsp sugar

1¼ cups water

3¾ cups bread flour, plus extra for kneading

1½ tsp salt

1 Sprinkle the yeast and sugar into ½ cup of the water in a bowl. Let stand for 5 minutes; stir to dissolve. Mix the flour and salt in a large bowl. Make a well in the center of the flour and pour in the dissolved yeast.

2 Pour about half of the remaining water into the well. Mix in the flour. Stir in the reserved water, as needed, to form a firm, moist dough.

3 Turn the dough out onto a well-floured work surface. Knead until smooth and elastic, about 10 minutes. As you knead the dough, gradually work in as much additional flour as you can comfortably knead – this dough should be very stiff and firm.

4 Put the dough in a lightly oiled bowl, turning the dough to coat, and cover with a dish towel. Let rise until doubled in size, about 1 hour. Punch down, then let rest for 10 minutes.

5 Cut the dough into eight equal pieces. Shape each piece into a ball (see page 55). Form each ball into a ring by inserting a floured finger into the center of each one.

6 Work the finger in a circle to stretch and widen the hole. Then twirl the ring around the index finger of one hand and the thumb of the other hand until the hole is about ⅓ of the bagel's diameter.

7 Place the bagels on a lightly oiled baking sheet, then cover with a damp dish towel and let rest for 10 minutes.

8 Bring a large pan of water to a boil, then reduce the heat to allow the water to simmer. Use a perforated skimmer to carefully lower the bagels into the water in batches of two to three at a time. Boil according to the instructions, below.

9 Transfer the drained bagels to a lightly oiled baking sheet. Bake in the preheated oven for 20 minutes, until golden. Cool on a wire rack.

Rising
1 hour
(see pages 50–51)

Oven temperature
425°F

Baking
20 minutes
Steam optional
(see page 63)

Yield
8 bagels

Yeast alternative
1 cake (0.6oz) yeast
(see page 41)

BOILING THE BAGELS

Boil each batch of 2–3 bagels, uncovered, until they rise to the surface, about 1 minute, turning them once. Remove the bagels from the water, using a perforated skimmer, and drain.

SALZBREZELN
PRETZELS

In their native Germany, these twisted ring-shaped and salt-sprinkled breads are traditionally eaten as a snack with beer, but they make an especially savory and tasty accompaniment to many drinks. There are two main sorts of pretzel—hard and crisp or light and chewy. If you prefer your pretzel hard and crisp, omit the final rising after the dough has been shaped.

INGREDIENTS

2 tsp dry yeast

1¼ cups water

3¼ cups bread flour

1½ tsp salt

egg glaze, made with 1 egg and 1 tbsp water (see page 58)

sesame seeds, poppy seeds, or coarse sea salt, for topping

1 Sprinkle the yeast into ½ cup of the water in a bowl. Let stand for 5 minutes; stir to dissolve. Mix the flour and salt in a large bowl. Make a well in the center and pour in the dissolved yeast.

2 Use a wooden spoon to draw enough of the flour into the dissolved yeast to form a soft paste. Cover the bowl with a dish towel and let "sponge" until frothy and risen, about 20 minutes.

3 Mix in the flour. Stir in the remaining water, as needed, to form a stiff, sticky dough.

4 Turn the dough out onto a lightly floured work surface. Knead until smooth and elastic, about 10 minutes.

5 Put the dough in a bowl and cover with a dish towel. Let rise until doubled in size, 1½–2 hours. Punch down, then let rest for 10 minutes.

6 Divide the dough into eight pieces. Shape each piece into a round roll and then into an oval (*see page 55*). Roll each oval backward and forward with your fingers, along the dough, until it forms a strip about 16 inches long and is 1 inch thick in the middle and ¼ inch at each end.

7 To shape the dough, follow the instructions, below. Place the pretzels on a lightly floured baking sheet and cover with a dish towel. Proof until each piece has doubled in size, about 45 minutes.

8 Brush the egg glaze over each pretzel and sprinkle with the topping of your choice. Bake in the preheated oven for 15–20 minutes, until golden brown. Cool on a wire rack.

VARIATION
Salzstangen
(Salted Breadsticks)

• Make one quantity Salzbrezeln dough up to step 6.
• Divide the dough into two equal pieces, then roll each piece into a 12-inch square.
• Using a sharp knife, cut each square in half diagonally, then in half again to form eight triangles. Starting at the widest end, roll up each triangle tightly like a cigar.
• Place the rolled sticks on two lightly floured baking sheets and cover with a dish towel. Proof until doubled in size, about 40 minutes. Preheat the oven to 425°F.
• Continue as directed in step 8.

To begin
Sponge method
Time: 20 minutes
(*see page 44*)

Rising
1½–2 hours
(*see pages 50–51*)

Proofing
45 minutes
(*see page 57*)

Oven temperature
425°F

Baking
15–20 minutes
Steam optional
(*see page 63*)

Yield
8 pretzels

Yeast alternative
1 cake (0.6oz) yeast
(*see page 41*)

FORMING THE PRETZELS

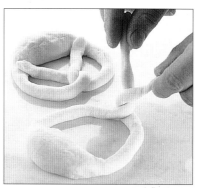

Once the dough has been divided and shaped into strips, pick up the two ends of each strip to make a loop. Cross the ends over twice and then press them down on either side of the dough loop; repeat these actions with each strip of dough.

SOURDOUGHS & OTHER BREADS USING STARTERS

A STARTER ADDS TO THE FLAVOR and the texture of a loaf. It is made from a small amount of flour, water, and prepared yeast that is left to ferment at room temperature (*see pages 42–43*). The only difference between starter breads and basic breads is in the time required to make them. The methods are the same. Rustic-style sourdough breads are made with starters that require an initial fermentation of at least 48 hours. This produces a bread with a pleasantly sour aroma, hearty texture, and chewy crust. The longer a starter is left to ferment, the more pronounced these qualities become in the finished loaf. All starters have to be refrigerated after five days and will keep for up to two weeks. They should be replenished with equal amounts of flour and water after use. In Italy, a starter, or *biga*, traditionally ferments for at least 12 hours. This produces a bread with a lightly fermented flavor, a Champagne-like aroma, and an open, porous texture. In France, a starter, or *poolish*, traditionally ferments for at least two hours. This shorter fermentation produces a bread with a less yeasty taste, nutty aroma, and springy texture; it has some of the chewiness of a sourdough loaf counterbalanced with the lightness of a basic bread.

PAIN DE CAMPAGNE

PAIN DE CAMPAGNE
FRENCH COUNTRY-STYLE BREAD WITH A SOURDOUGH STARTER

A classic French loaf, this bread has all the signature qualities of the popular rustic-style sourdough breads—tangy flavor, springy texture, and chewy crust. French bakers traditionally proof the shaped dough in a basket. The basket supports the dough, allowing it to retain its shape before baking. Place the dough in a basket, about 8 inches in diameter, lined with a well-floured dish towel. Proof as directed in step 7.

PROOFING IN A BASKET

INGREDIENTS
for the starter

2 tsp dry yeast
1¼ cups water
2 cups bread flour

for the dough

1 tsp dry yeast
1 cup water
½ cup rye flour
2⅓ cups bread flour
1½ tsp salt

1 To make the starter Sprinkle the yeast into the water in a large jar. Let stand for 5 minutes; stir to dissolve. Stir in the flour using a wooden spoon. Cover the jar with a dish towel and let ferment at room temperature for at least 2 days or, at most, 3 days. Stir the mixture twice a day; it will be bubbly and pleasantly sour-smelling.

2 To make the dough Sprinkle the yeast into the water in a small bowl. Let stand for 5 minutes; stir to dissolve. Mix the flours and the salt together in a large bowl and make a well in the center.

3 Spoon 1 cup of the starter into a liquid measuring cup. Add it to the flour well and pour in the dissolved yeast. Reserve and replenish the remaining starter (*see far right*) in the same jar for the next time you make bread.

4 Mix in the flour from the sides of the well to form a stiff, sticky dough. Add more water, 1 tablespoon at a time, if the mixture is too dry.

5 Turn the dough out onto a lightly floured work surface. Knead until smooth and elastic, about 10 minutes.

6 Put the dough in a clean bowl and cover with a dish towel. Let rise for 2 hours. Punch down; let rest for 10 minutes.

7 Shape the dough into a round loaf (*see page 54*). Place on a floured baking sheet. Cover with a dish towel and proof until doubled in size, about 1½ hours.

8 Dust the loaf with flour. Cut three parallel slashes (*see page 62*), ¼ inch deep, across the top of the loaf, then three more in the opposite direction. Bake in the preheated oven for 1 hour, until golden brown and hollow sounding when tapped underneath. Cool on a wire rack.

VARIATIONS
Couronne (Crown or Ring Loaf)
(see page 12 for illustration)

• Make one quantity Pain de Campagne dough up to step 7.
• Shape the dough into a ring shape (*see page 56*).
• Cover the loaf with a dish towel and proof until doubled in size, about 1½ hours. Preheat the oven to 425°F.
• Bake for 45 minutes, until hollow sounding when tapped underneath. Cool on a wire rack.

Pain Tordu
(see page 13 for illustration)

• Make one quantity Pain de Campagne dough up to step 7.
• Shape the dough into a cylinder, 14 inches long. With the handle of a wooden spoon, make an indentation down the center.
• Twist the dough as if wringing out a cloth. Place it on a floured baking sheet, dust with flour, and proof. Preheat the oven to 425°F.
• Bake for 1 hour, until hollow sounding when tapped underneath. Cool on a wire rack.

To begin
Starter
Time: 2–3 days
(*see page 43*)

Rising
2 hours
(*see pages 50–51*)

Proofing
1½ hours
(*see page 57*)

Oven temperature
425°F

Baking
1 hour
Steam optional
(*see page 63*)

Yield
1 loaf

Yeast alternative
For the starter:
1 cake (0.6oz) yeast
For the dough:
⅛ cake (0.6oz-sized) yeast (*see page 41*)

MAINTAINING THE STARTER
Place the remaining starter in the jar and replenish it with an equal amount of flour and water. If you remove 1 cup of starter to make this recipe, add ½ cup water and 1 cup flour to the jar. This will allow you to keep the sourdough starter fermenting for the next time you make bread. Refer to page 43 for more detailed instructions.

SAN FRANCISCO SOURDOUGH

During the American gold rush, prospectors often carried a mixture of flour and water in a package strapped to their waists. The heat from their bodies fermented the mixture and created a natural leaven. This gave them the nickname "sourbellies." This tradition of sourdough baking has continued. San Franciscans claim that their city is the sourdough capital of North America.
If you wish to maintain the starter, follow the instructions on page 85. (See page 20 for an illustration of the bread.)

"OLD" DOUGH

INGREDIENTS
for the starter

3 tsp dry yeast

2 cups water

2¼ cups bread flour, sifted

for the dough

1¼ cups bread flour

⅔ cup whole-wheat flour

2 tsp salt

2½-inch ball "old" dough
(one piece from recipe below)

1 To make the starter Sprinkle yeast into the water in a large jar. Let stand for 5 minutes; stir to dissolve.

2 Stir the flour into the jar of dissolved yeast using a wooden spoon. Cover with a dish towel and ferment at room temperature for at least 3 days and at most 5 days before refrigerating. Stir the mixture twice a day; it will be bubbly and pleasantly sour-smelling.

3 To make the dough Mix the flours and salt in a large bowl. Make a well in the center. Spoon 2 cups of the starter into a liquid measuring cup. Replenish the remaining starter for the next time you make bread (see page 85). Tear the "old" dough into tiny pieces, then add the starter and the "old" dough pieces to the flour well.

4 Mix in the flour to form a firm but moist dough. Add more water as needed, 1 tablespoon at a time, if the dough is too dry.

5 Turn the dough out onto a lightly floured work surface. Knead until smooth and elastic, about 10 minutes.

6 Put the dough in a clean bowl and cover with a dish towel. Let rise until doubled in size, about 2 hours. Punch down, then let rest for 10 minutes.

7 Pinch off a 2½ oz piece of the dough for your next breadmaking. Wrap the piece of dough loosely in waxed paper and foil, and refrigerate or freeze the dough until the next time you make bread (see page 43).

8 Shape the remaining dough into a round loaf (see page 54). Place on a floured baking sheet. Cover with a dish towel and proof until doubled in size, about 1½ hours.

9 Cut three parallel slashes (see page 62), about ¼ inch deep, across the top of the loaf, then three more slashes in the opposite direction to make a crisscross pattern. Dust with flour and bake in the preheated oven for 1 hour, until golden and hollow sounding when tapped underneath. Let cool on a wire rack.

 To begin
Starter
Time: 3–5 days
(see page 43)

"Old" dough
Time: 3½ hours
(to make ahead, see page 43)

 Rising
2 hours
(see pages 50–51)

 Proofing
1½ hours
(see page 57)

 Oven temperature
425°F

 Baking
1 hour
Steam optional
(see page 63)

 Yield
1 loaf

 Yeast alternative
For the starter:
1½ cakes
(0.6oz-sized) yeast
(see page 41)

RECIPE FOR "OLD" DOUGH
INGREDIENTS

½ tsp dry yeast or ⅛ of a cake (0.6oz-sized) yeast

4 tbsp lukewarm water

¼ cup bread flour

1 Sprinkle the yeast into the water in a large bowl. Let stand for 5 minutes, then stir with a wooden spoon to dissolve.

2 Mix the flour into the dissolved yeast to form a stiff, sticky dough. Turn the dough out onto a lightly floured work surface. Knead until smooth and elastic, about 10 minutes.

3 Put the dough in a lightly oiled bowl and cover with a dish towel. Let rise for 3 hours. Punch down. Divide the dough into two equal pieces. Wrap one piece for future use and add the other piece to the flour well in step 3 of the recipe.

4 "Old" dough can be prepared in advance and frozen (see page 43) or refrigerated. Wrap loosely in waxed paper and foil, allowing room for the dough to expand slightly. Defrost or remove from the refrigerator 1½ hours before use.

PANE DI SEMOLA
SEMOLINA BREAD

This open-textured bread comes from Puglia, a region of southern Italy, and is commonly known as Pugliese. Its open texture is good for absorbing oil – making it especially popular to use for Bruschetta (see page 156). Fields of semolina grow profusely in the scorching sun of the region. The semolina flour gives this bread a distinctive golden color and a crisp crust.

INGREDIENTS
for the starter

¼ tsp dry yeast

⅔ cup water

1 cup bread flour

for the dough

1½ tsp dry yeast

¼ cup water

1 cup bread flour

1⅔ cups semolina or durum wheat flour, plus extra to dust

2 tsp salt

2 tbsp olive oil

1 To make the starter Sprinkle the yeast into the water in a bowl. Let stand for 5 minutes; stir to dissolve. Add the flour and mix to form a thick batter. Cover with a dish towel and let ferment at room temperature for 12–24 hours.

2 To make the dough Sprinkle the yeast into ½ cup of the water in a small bowl. Let stand for 5 minutes; stir to dissolve. Mix the flours and salt in a large bowl. Make a well in the center and pour in the dissolved yeast, the oil, and the starter.

3 Mix in the flour. Pour in the remaining water, as needed, to form a soft, sticky dough.

4 Turn the dough out onto a lightly floured work surface. Knead the dough until smooth and elastic, about 10 minutes.

5 Put the dough in a clean, lightly oiled bowl. Let rise until doubled in size, about 1½–2 hours. Punch down the dough and chafe for 5 minutes (*see page 51*), then let rest for 10 minutes.

6 Divide the dough into two pieces. Shape each piece into a round loaf (*see page 54*). Place the loaves on an oiled baking sheet dusted with semolina flour.

7 Flatten each loaf with the palm of your hand and sprinkle with semolina flour. Cover with a dish towel and proof until both loaves are doubled in size, about 1½ hours.

8 Bake in the preheated oven for 30 minutes, until lightly golden and hollow sounding when tapped underneath. Cool on a wire rack.

To begin
Starter
Time: 12–24 hours
(*see page 42*)

Rising
1½–2 hours
(*see pages 50–51*)

Proofing
1½ hours
(*see page 57*)

Oven temperature
400°F

Baking
30 minutes
Steam optional
(*see page 63*)

Yield
2 loaves

Yeast alternative
For the starter:
⅛ of a cake
(0.6oz-sized) yeast
For the dough:
¼ of a cake
(0.6oz-sized) yeast
(*see page 41*)

PANE DI PRATO
TRADITIONAL SALTLESS TUSCAN BREAD

*T*his typical Tuscan bread, also known as Pane Toscano, *is made without salt. The absence of salt has a historical explanation. During the Middle Ages, Tuscany's neighboring provinces controlled the Italian salt market, levying a heavy salt tax. Unwilling to submit to their rivals, the Tuscans created breads made without salt. Such breads have a yeasty flavor, but quickly become stale. Tuscan cooks have developed a tradition of dishes using stale bread (see pages 156–161).*

INGREDIENTS
for the starter

3½ tsp dry yeast

⅔ cup water

1 cup plus 2 tbsp bread flour

for the dough

2¼ cups bread flour

1¼ cups water

1 **To make the starter** Sprinkle the yeast into the water in a bowl. Let stand for 5 minutes; stir to dissolve. Add the flour and mix to form a thick paste. Cover with a dish towel and let ferment at room temperature for at least 12 hours.

2 **To make the dough** Put the flour in a large bowl. Make a well in the center of the flour and add the starter. Pour in about half of the water. Mix in the flour from the sides of the well, then stir in the reserved water to form a wet, batterlike dough.

3 Cover the bowl with a dish towel and let rise until doubled in size, about 40 minutes.

4 Turn the dough out onto a well-floured work surface. Use floured hands and a plastic dough scraper to knead the dough until smooth and elastic, about 10 minutes (*see below, right*). Work in additional flour only if necessary to achieve a manageable, but still very moist dough.

5 Divide the dough into two equal pieces. Handle the dough carefully so as not to deflate it. Shape each piece into an oval loaf (*see page 55*). Place on an oiled baking sheet and cover with a dish towel. Proof until doubled in size, about 15–20 minutes.

6 Strain a light dusting of flour over the two loaves. Bake in the preheated oven for 35 minutes, until lightly golden and hollow sounding when tapped underneath. Cool on a wire rack.

 To begin
Starter
Time: 12 hours
(*see page 42*)

 Rising
40 minutes
(*see pages 50–51*)

 Proofing
15–20 minutes
(*see page 57*)

 Oven temperature
375°F

 Baking
35 minutes
Steam optional
(*see page 63*)

 Yield
2 small loaves

 Yeast alternative
For the starter:
1¼ cakes
(0.6oz-sized) yeast
(*see page 41*)

KNEADING A WET DOUGH

A well-floured work surface and hands are necessary when kneading a wet, batterlike dough. Handle the dough with slow, gentle movements. Use a plastic dough scraper to carefully push and turn it. After kneading, the dough should still be soft and pliable.

PANE CASALINGO
ITALIAN "HOUSEHOLD" BREAD

In Italy, casalingo describes the very best of family cooking, passed down from one generation to the next. Pane Casalingo literally means "home-baked bread" and one that is never found in bakeries. It is common all over Italy, from north to south, which is very unusual in the fiercely proud regional cooking of Italy. We like to think of it as a bread without boundaries. The starter is uniquely made with malt and milk. This combination speeds up the fermentation of the yeast, which gives the bread a slightly yeasty flavor.

INGREDIENTS
for the starter

1¼ tsp dry yeast

¼ cup water

½ cup lukewarm milk

1 tsp malt extract

1½ cups bread flour

for the dough

1¼ tsp dry yeast

¼ cup plus 2 tbsp water

2¼ cups bread flour

2 tsp salt

1 **To make the starter** Sprinkle the yeast into the water and milk in a bowl. Let stand for 5 minutes, then add the malt extract and stir to dissolve. Add the flour and mix to form a thick paste. Cover with a dish towel and let ferment for 12 hours.

2 **To make the dough** Sprinkle the yeast into ½ cup of the water in a bowl. Let stand for 5 minutes; stir to dissolve. Mix the flour and the salt in a large bowl. Make a well in the center and add the dissolved yeast and the starter.

3 Pour half of the remaining water into the well. Mix in the flour. Stir in the reserved water, as needed, to form a soft dough.

4 Turn the dough out onto a well-floured work surface. Knead for 5 minutes. Cover with a dish towel, let rest for 10 minutes, then knead for 5 minutes longer.

5 Put the dough in a clean bowl and cover with a dish towel. Let rise until tripled in size, about 2 hours. Punch down and chafe for 5 minutes (*see page 51*), then let rest for 10 minutes.

6 Shape the dough into a round loaf (*see page 54*). Place on an oiled baking sheet. Cover with a dish towel and proof until doubled in size, about 1½ hours.

7 Dust with flour. Cut three parallel slashes (*see page 62*), ¼ inch deep, across the top of the loaf, then three more in the opposite direction to make a crisscross pattern. Bake in the preheated oven for 50 minutes, until hollow sounding when tapped underneath. Cool on a wire rack.

 To begin
Starter
Time: 12 hours
(*see page 42*)

 Rising
2 hours
(*see pages 50–51*)

 Proofing
1½ hours
(*see page 57*)

 Oven temperature
400°F

 Baking
50 minutes
Steam optional
(*see page 63*)

 Yield
1 loaf

 Yeast alternative
For the starter:
¼ of a cake
(0.6oz-sized) yeast
For the dough:
¼ of a cake
(0.6oz-sized) yeast
(*see page 41*)

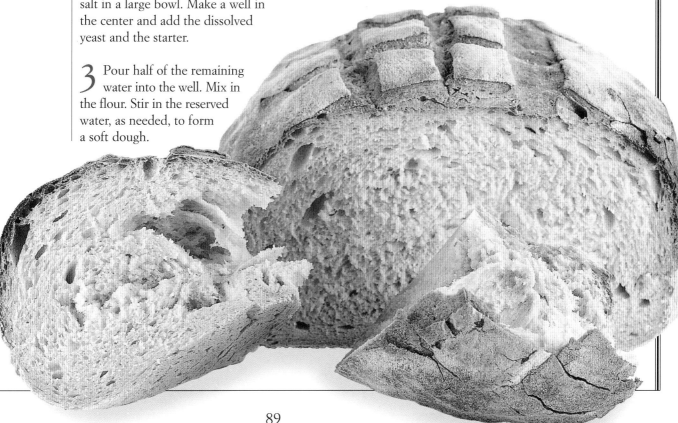

CIABATTA
ITALIAN "SLIPPER" BREAD

Ciabatta *was given its name because the bread resembles a well-worn slipper. It is the prolonged rising and high liquid content that produce this very light bread, with its uniquely open and porous texture. An authentic* Ciabatta *requires a very wet dough that can be tricky to handle and must be started a day in advance. Do not be tempted to add extra flour to make the dough more manageable, and avoid overhandling the dough at all costs. After its long rise, the dough must be handled with a very light touch ("like a baby," as they say in Italy), so that all the precious air bubbles are not broken.*

INGREDIENTS
for the starter
½ tsp dry yeast

⅔ cup water

3 tbsp milk

¼ tsp honey or sugar

1 cup plus 2 tbsp bread flour

for the dough
½ tsp dry yeast

1 cup water

½ tbsp olive oil

2½ cups bread flour

1½ tsp salt

1 To make the starter Sprinkle the yeast into the water and milk in a large bowl. Let stand for 5 minutes, then add the honey or sugar and stir to dissolve.

2 Mix in the flour to form a loose batter. Cover the bowl with a dish towel and let rise for 12 hours or overnight.

3 To make the dough Sprinkle the yeast into the water in a small bowl. Let stand for 5 minutes, then stir to dissolve. Add the dissolved yeast and olive oil to the starter and mix well.

4 Mix in the flour and salt to form a wet, sticky dough. Beat steadily with a wooden spoon for 5 minutes; the dough will become springy and start to pull away from the sides of the bowl, but will remain too soft to knead.

5 Cover the dough with a dish towel. Let rise until tripled in size and full of air bubbles, about 3 hours. Do not punch down the dough. Generously flour two baking sheets and have ready extra flour to dip your hands in.

6 Use a dough scraper to divide the dough in half while in the bowl. Scoop half the dough out of the bowl onto one of the heavily floured baking sheets.

7 Use well-floured hands to pull and stretch the dough to form a roughly rectangular loaf, about 12 inches long. Dust the loaf and your hands again with flour. Neaten and plump up the loaf by running your fingers down each side and gently tucking under the edges of the dough (*see below*).

8 Repeat step 7 with the other half of the dough. Leave the two loaves uncovered to proof for about 20 minutes; the loaves will spread out as well as rise.

9 Bake in the preheated oven for 30 minutes, until risen, golden, and hollow sounding when tapped underneath. Cool on a wire rack.

 To begin
Starter
Time: 12 hours
or overnight
(*see page 42*)

 Rising
3 hours
(*see pages 50–51*)

 Proofing
20 minutes
(*see page 57*)

 Oven temperature
425°F

 Baking
30 minutes
Steam optional
(*see page 63*)

 Yield
2 loaves

 Yeast alternative
For the starter:
⅛ of a cake
(0.6oz-sized) yeast
For the dough:
⅛ of a cake
(0.6oz-sized) yeast
(*see page 41*)

SHAPING CIABATTA

Use well-floured hands to neaten and plump up the loaf by running your fingers down each side and gently tucking under the edges of the dough.

LANDBROT
GERMAN COUNTRY-STYLE RYE BREAD

Rye is the most important of all grain crops in Germany, and German bakers are the undisputed masters of rye breads. Landbrot translates literally as "bread of the land," and it is the German equivalent of Pain de Campagne. *It is baked throughout Germany, and although there are regional differences in color and texture, because the proportions of rye to wheat vary, it is usually dusted with flour. (See page 18 for an illustration of the bread.)*

INGREDIENTS
for the starter

½ tsp dry yeast

3 tbsp water

⅓ cup bread flour

1 tbsp milk

for the dough

1½ tsp dry yeast

1½ cups water

3½ cups rye flour

¼ cup bread flour

2 tsp salt

1 **To make the starter** Sprinkle the yeast into the water in a bowl. Let stand for 5 minutes; stir to dissolve. Mix in the flour and milk. Cover with a dish towel and ferment at room temperature for 12–18 hours. The mixture will be bubbly and pleasantly sour-smelling.

2 **To make the dough** Sprinkle the yeast into 1 cup of the water in a bowl. Let stand for 5 minutes; stir to dissolve. Mix the flours in a large bowl. Make a well in the center and add the dissolved yeast and starter.

3 Use a wooden spoon to draw enough of the flour into the starter mixture to form a thick batter. Cover the bowl with a dish towel and let "sponge" until frothy and risen, 12–18 hours.

4 Add the salt to the fermented batter. Mix in the flour. Stir in the reserved water, as needed, to form a stiff, sticky dough.

5 Turn the dough out onto a lightly floured work surface. Knead until smooth and elastic, about 10 minutes. Let rest for 10 minutes.

6 Shape the dough into a round loaf (*see page 54*). Place on a floured baking sheet. Dust with flour. Cut one slash, ½ inch deep, across the top of the loaf, then another in the opposite direction to make an "X" (*see page 62*).

7 Cover with a dish towel and proof until doubled in size, about 1½ hours.

8 Bake in the preheated oven for 1¼ hours, until hollow sounding when tapped. Cool on a wire rack.

VARIATIONS
Seeded German Rye Bread
• Combine 2 tablespoons each flaxseeds, sesame seeds, and pumpkin seeds in a food processor. Using the pulse button, process until roughly chopped. Alternatively, grind by hand using a mortar and pestle.
• Make one quantity Landbrot dough up to step 4.
• Add the seed mixture with the salt to the fermented batter. Continue as directed in steps 4–5.
• Shape the dough for a greased 9 x 5 x 3-inch loaf pan (*see page 53*).
• Proof as directed in step 7. Preheat the oven to 400°F.
• Brush with milk and sprinkle with whole flaxseeds, sesame seeds, and pumpkin seeds.
• Bake as directed in step 8.

Rye Bread with Caraway Seeds
• Make one quantity Landbrot dough, adding ½ teaspoon caraway seeds to the starter in step 1.
• Shape the dough for a greased 9 x 5 x 3-inch loaf pan (*see page 53*).
• Proof as directed in step 7. Preheat the oven to 400°F.
• Brush with milk and sprinkle 2 tablespoons rye flakes on the top.
• Bake as directed in step 8.

To begin
Starter
Time: 12–18 hours
(*see page 42*)

Sponge method
Time: 12–18 hours
(*see page 44*)

Proofing
1½ hours
(*see page 57*)

Oven temperature
400°F

Baking
1¼ hours
Steam optional
(*see page 63*)

Yield
1 loaf

Yeast alternative
For the starter:
¼ of a cake
(0.6oz-sized) yeast
For the dough:
⅛ of a cake
(0.6oz-sized) yeast
(*see page 41*)

PAIN DE SEIGLE

FRENCH RYE BREAD

In France, rye bread originated in mountainous regions, such as the Alps, the Pyrenees, and Vosges, where it was a staple, everyday bread. Today, rye bread is eaten more infrequently, but it is always served, thinly sliced and thickly buttered, as an accompaniment to oysters or the gargantuan plateau de fruits de mer, which is a specialty of the brasseries of Paris.

INGREDIENTS

for the starter

2 tsp dry yeast
⅔ cup water
1 cup bread flour

for the dough

½ cup bread flour
3 cups rye flour
2 tsp salt
1 cup water

1 To make the starter Sprinkle the yeast into the water in a bowl. Let stand for 5 minutes; stir to dissolve. Add the flour and mix to form a thick batter. Cover with a dish towel and leave for 2 hours.

2 To make the dough Mix the flours and the salt together in a large bowl. Make a well in the center and pour in the starter and half of the water.

3 Mix in the flour. Stir in the remaining water to form a fairly moist, sticky dough.

4 Turn the dough out onto a lightly floured work surface. Knead the dough until smooth and elastic, about 10 minutes.

5 Put the dough in a clean bowl and cover with a dish towel. Let rise until doubled in size, about 1 hour. Punch down, then let rest for 10 minutes.

6 Divide the dough into two equal pieces and shape each piece into a long loaf (*see pages 52–53*), about 12 inches in length. Place the loaves on a floured baking sheet and let rest for 5 minutes.

7 Dust the loaves lightly with flour. Cut six or seven short, parallel slashes, ¼ inch deep, at ½-inch intervals, down both sides of the loaves (*see page 62*). Cover with a dish towel and proof until doubled in size, about 1½ hours.

8 Bake in the preheated oven for 45 minutes, until hollow sounding when tapped underneath. Cool on a wire rack.

To begin
Starter
Time: 2 hours
(*see page 42*)

Rising
1 hour
(*see pages 50–51*)

Proofing
1½ hours
(*see page 57*)

Oven temperature
400°F

Baking
45 minutes
Steam optional
(*see page 63*)

Yield
2 small loaves

Yeast alternative
1 cake (0.6oz) yeast
(*see page 41*))

FLAVORED BREADS

ADDING FLAVORINGS TO A BASIC DOUGH ALLOWS THE BAKER TO VARY THE TASTE, TEXTURE, AND COLOR OF A BREAD. FLAVORINGS ARE EITHER INCORPORATED DURING MIXING OR ADDED TO A KNEADED DOUGH. LIGHT INGREDIENTS, SUCH AS HERBS AND SPICES, WHICH DO NOT INHIBIT THE DOUGH'S RISING, ARE ADDED WITH THE FLOUR AT THE MIXING STAGE. MOIST INGREDIENTS, SUCH AS GRATED OR PURÉED VEGETABLES OR COOKED WHOLE GRAINS, WHICH ALSO SUPPLY SOME OF THE DOUGH'S LIQUID CONTENT, ARE ALSO ADDED BEFORE RISING. HEAVIER INGREDIENTS, SUCH AS NUTS, TEND TO BE KNEADED IN AFTER THE DOUGH HAS RISEN IN ORDER NOT TO HINDER THE ACTION OF THE YEAST. ALTERNATIVELY, A BASIC DOUGH CAN BE TOPPED OR FILLED JUST BEFORE BAKING.

LEFT **CARROT BREAD IN A VARIETY OF FLAVOR VARIATIONS**

CARROT BREAD

Adding shredded raw vegetables to a basic dough will enhance a bread's color, texture, and flavor. We find that grated carrots make a most attractive savory loaf, but grated raw beets contribute the most dramatic coloring. This excellent crusty loaf with an orange-flecked, spongy crumb is universally popular. Both grated raw vegetables and cooked vegetable purées can be worked into this dough with great success.

INGREDIENTS

| 2 tsp dry yeast |
| 1½ cups water |
| 3¼ cups bread flour |
| 2 tsp salt |
| 2¼ cups grated carrots |
| 1 tbsp unsalted butter, melted |

1 Sprinkle the yeast into ½ cup of the water. Let stand for 5 minutes; stir to dissolve.

2 Mix the flour and salt in a large bowl. Make a well in the center and pour in the dissolved yeast. Add the carrots and butter to the well. Mix in the flour. Stir in the remaining water, as needed, to form a moist, crumbly dough.

3 Turn the dough out onto a lightly floured work surface. Knead the dough until smooth but still sticky, about 10 minutes.

4 Put the dough in a clean bowl and cover with a dish towel. Let rise until doubled in size, about 1–1½ hours. Punch down, then let rest for 10 minutes.

5 Shape the dough into a round loaf (see page 54). Place on a floured baking sheet and cover with a dish towel. Proof until doubled in size, about 45 minutes.

6 Bake in the preheated oven for 45 minutes, until golden and hollow sounding when tapped underneath. Cool on a wire rack.

VARIATIONS
Spinach Bread
• Immerse 5 cups spinach in rapidly boiling water.
• When the water returns to a boil, drain and rinse the spinach in cold water; squeeze dry.
• In a food processor or blender, purée the spinach, about 1 minute.
• Put the purée in a measuring cup and pour in enough water to make up a volume of 1 cup.
• Make one quantity Carrot Bread dough up to step 4, replacing the grated carrot and remaining water with the spinach purée liquid in step 2. Pour the spinach purée liquid into the flour well to form a moist, crumbly dough.
• Continue as directed in steps 4–6.

Beet Bread
• Make one quantity Carrot Bread dough up to step 4, replacing the grated carrot with grated raw beets in step 2.
• Continue as directed in steps 4–6.

Herb Bread
• Make one quantity Carrot Bread dough up to step 4, replacing the grated carrot with a handful of finely chopped herbs in step 2. Choose parsley for color, and use it in combination with either rosemary and thyme, or chives and marjoram.
• Continue as directed in steps 4–6.

Chili Bread
• Make one quantity Carrot Bread dough up to step 4, replacing the carrots with 3 teaspoons crushed red pepper flakes. Mix with flour and salt in step 2.
• Continue as directed in steps 4–6.

Onion and Caraway Bread
• Melt 4 tablespoons butter in a pan over medium heat. Add 1 onion, chopped. Cook for 10 minutes, until soft and golden.
• Make one quantity Carrot Bread dough up to step 4, replacing the carrots with the onion and 1 tablespoon caraway seeds.

 Rising
1½–2 hours
(see pages 50–51)

 Proofing
45 minutes
(see page 57)

 Oven temperature
400°F

 Baking
45 minutes
Steam optional
(see page 63)

 Yield
1 loaf

Yeast alternative
1 cake (0.6oz) yeast
(see page 41)

PUMPKIN BREAD

This slightly sweet, light-textured bread has a soft crust and a rich, golden crumb. When you are unable to find fresh pumpkins at the supermarket, canned pumpkin purée will work just as well. Use water as a substitute for the reserved cooking liquid. Acorn or butternut squash can be used as an alternative to pumpkin.

PUMPKIN BREAD

INGREDIENTS

1½lbs pumpkin, peeled, seeded, and cut into pieces, or 1¼ cups canned pumpkin purée

2 tsp dry yeast

2 tsp honey

4 cups bread flour

2 tsp salt

egg glaze, made with 1 egg yolk and 1 tbsp milk (see page 58)

2 tbsp pumpkin seeds, to decorate

1 Bring a pan of salted water to a boil. Add the pumpkin and simmer steadily until soft and cooked through, about 20 minutes. Drain the pumpkin well and reserve the cooking liquid.

2 Mash the pumpkin thoroughly and strain or purée in a food processor or blender, about 2 minutes. Let the pumpkin purée and reserved cooking liquid cool until lukewarm.

3 Sprinkle the yeast into ¼ cup of the reserved cooking liquid (or water, if using canned pumpkin purée). Let stand for 5 minutes; add the honey and stir to dissolve.

4 Mix the flour and salt in a large bowl. Make a well in the center and pour in the dissolved yeast and honey, then add the pumpkin purée.

5 Mix in the flour gradually to form a fairly firm, coarse, sticky dough. If the mixture is too dry, add a few tablespoons of the pumpkin cooking liquid (or water, if using a can of pumpkin purée).

6 Turn the dough out onto a lightly floured work surface. Knead until very smooth, silky, and elastic, about 10 minutes.

7 Put the dough in a clean bowl and cover with a dish towel. Let rise until doubled in size, about 1½ hours. Punch down, then let rest for 10 minutes.

8 Shape the dough into a round loaf (*see page 54*). Place on an oiled baking sheet and cover with a dish towel. Proof until doubled in size, about 1 hour.

9 Brush the dough with the egg glaze and sprinkle pumpkin seeds over the top. Bake in the preheated oven for 40 minutes, until golden colored and hollow sounding when tapped underneath. Cool on a wire rack.

 Rising
1½ hours
(*see pages 50–51*)

 Proofing
1 hour
(*see page 57*)

 Oven temperature
425°F

 Baking
40 minutes
Steam optional
(*see page 63*)

 Yield
1 loaf

 Yeast alternative
1 cake (0.6oz) yeast
(*see page 41*)

MIXING IN THE FLAVORING

Add the pumpkin purée directly to the flour along with the dissolved yeast.

PAIN AU FROMAGE
CHEESE HEARTH BREAD

This cheese-enriched, crusty bread from southern France was traditionally baked in a hearth on the dying embers of a fire. It is a perfect casse-croute *(which means "snack," or literally "break-crust"), served with a few black olives, a slice of* jambon de pays *(country ham), and a glass of red wine. Try Roquefort or goat cheese, crumbled rather than grated, as an alternative to Gruyère.*

PAIN AU FROMAGE

INGREDIENTS

2 tsp dry yeast
1¼ cups water
3¼ cups bread flour
1½ tsp salt
1 tbsp olive oil
2¼ cups grated Gruyère plus extra for topping, optional

1 Sprinkle the yeast into ½ cup of the water in a bowl. Let stand for 5 minutes; stir to dissolve. Mix the flour and salt in a large bowl. Make a well in the center of the flour and pour in the dissolved yeast and olive oil.

2 Use a wooden spoon to draw enough of the flour into the dissolved yeast to form a thick paste. Cover the bowl with a dish towel; let "sponge" until frothy and risen, about 20 minutes.

3 Pour about half of the remaining water into the well. Mix in the flour. Stir in the reserved water, as needed, to form a firm, moist dough.

4 Turn the dough out onto a lightly floured work surface. Knead until smooth and elastic, about 10 minutes. Knead in the grated cheese (*see page 99*).

5 Put the dough in a clean bowl and cover with a dish towel. Let rise until doubled in size, about 1½ hours. Punch down, then let rest for 10 minutes.

6 Divide the dough into four equal pieces by flattening it into a round and cutting it into triangular quarters; let rest for 10 minutes.

7 Roll out each piece of dough into a flat, oval shape, about ¼ inch thick. If the dough resists rolling out, let it rest for 1–2 minutes. Transfer the dough onto two greased baking sheets.

8 With a sharp knife, make five slashes through each piece of dough, beginning and ending each cut about 1 inch from the edge of the dough. Open up each slash by gently pulling the edges apart slightly. Cover with a dish towel and proof for 45 minutes.

9 Sprinkle with additional grated cheese, if desired. Bake in the preheated oven for 25–30 minutes, until crisp, golden, and hollow sounding when tapped underneath. Cool on a wire rack.

VARIATION
Pain aux Olives (Olive Hearth Bread)
• Make one quantity Pain au Fromage dough, replacing the Gruyère with 1⅓ cups roughly chopped, pitted green olives in step 4.
• Decorate the shaped dough with more sliced olives instead of the cheese before baking in step 9.

To begin
Sponge method
Time: 20 minutes
(*see page 44*)

Rising
1½ hours
(*see pages 50–51*)

Proofing
45 minutes
(*see page 57*)

Oven temperature
400°F

Baking
25–30 minutes
Steam optional
(*see page 63*)

Yield
4 loaves

Yeast alternative
1 cake (0.6oz) yeast
(*see page 41*)

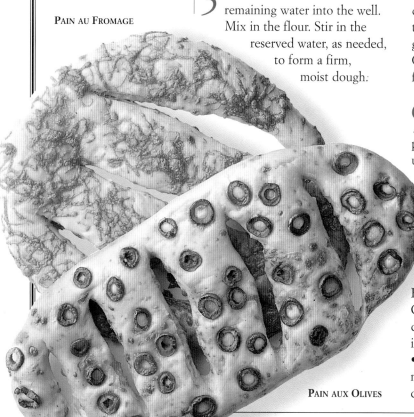
PAIN AUX OLIVES

PAIN AUX NOIX

WALNUT BREAD

Walnut bread goes especially well with goat cheese as well as the blue-veined sheeps-milk cheese, Roquefort. Any leftovers can be toasted to make Croutes *(see page 161) for a warm goat cheese salad.*

INGREDIENTS

2 tsp dry yeast
1½ cups water
2 cups bread flour
1 cup rye flour
1cup whole-wheat flour
2 tsp salt
1½ cups walnuts, roughly chopped

1 Sprinkle the yeast into ½ cup of the water in a bowl. Let stand for 5 minutes; stir to dissolve. Mix the flours and the salt in a bowl. Make a well in the center and pour in the dissolved yeast.

2 Use a wooden spoon to draw enough of the flour into the dissolved yeast to form a thick paste. Cover the bowl with a dish towel and let "sponge" until frothy and risen, about 20 minutes.

3 Pour about half of the remaining water into the well. Mix in the flour. Stir in the reserved water, as needed, to form a firm, moist dough.

4 Turn out onto a floured work surface. Knead until smooth and elastic, about 10 minutes. Add the walnuts at the end of kneading (*see below left and below right*).

5 Put the dough in a clean bowl and cover with a dish towel. Let rise until doubled in size, about 1½–2 hours. Punch down, then let rest for 10 minutes.

6 Shape the dough into an oblong loaf, about 10 inches long (*see page 52*). Place the shaped dough on a floured baking sheet; cover with a dish towel. Proof until doubled in size, about 45 minutes.

7 Bake in the preheated oven for 45 minutes–1 hour, until the loaf is hollow sounding when tapped underneath. Cool on a wire rack.

VARIATION

Pain aux Pruneaux et Noisette (Prune and Hazelnut Bread)

• Make one quantity Pain aux Noix dough up to step 5, replacing the walnuts with ½ cup each whole hazelnuts and quartered dried prunes.

• Let the dough rise until doubled in size, about 1½–2 hours. Punch down.

• Shape the dough as directed in step 6, then lightly press three whole prunes in a row on top of the loaf to decorate.

• Proof until doubled in size, about 45 minutes. Preheat the oven to 400°F.

• Bake as directed in step 7.

To begin
Sponge method
Time: 20 minutes
(*see page 44*)

Rising
1½–2 hours
(*see pages 50–51*)

Proofing
45 minutes
(*see page 57*)

Oven temperature
400°F

Baking
45 minutes–1 hour
Steam optional
(*see page 63*)

Yield
1 loaf

Yeast alternative
1 cake (0.6oz) yeast
(*see page 41*)

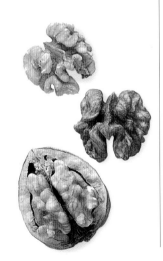

KNEADING IN COARSE INGREDIENTS

In step 4, let the dough rest for about 5 minutes so it will be easier to knead. Gently press the dough into a rectangle, about 1 inch thick. Sprinkle the walnuts over the surface. Fold the dough in half (see right).

Then gently knead the dough to evenly distribute the ingredients, about 2–4 minutes. The dough will separate and look crumbly before it comes together to form a smooth mass (see left).

MULTIGRAIN BREAD

MULTIGRAIN ROLLS

This healthy modern American classic has a nutty flavor and a crunchy texture as a result of the addition of seven ground and whole grains. Various brands of multigrain cereal are available at health-food stores, but you can mix your own. The eight whole grains used here are oats, brown rice, triticale (a hybrid of wheat and rye), rye, wheat, buckwheat, barley, and sesame seeds, but millet, soybean seeds, and flaxseeds are other possibilities.

INGREDIENTS

2 tsp dry yeast

1¼ cups water

2¼ cups bread flour

⅔ cup whole-wheat flour

⅔ cup multigrain cereal, ground

2 tsp salt

2 tbsp sunflower oil

2 tbsp honey

1⅓ cups cooked multigrain cereal, cooled

oat flakes or rolled oats, for topping

1 Grease a 9 x 5 x 3-inch loaf pan with oil. Sprinkle the yeast into the water in a bowl. Let stand for 5 minutes; stir to dissolve.

2 Mix the flours, ground grains, and salt in a large bowl. Make a well in the center and pour in the dissolved yeast, oil, honey, and cooked grains. Stir in the flour to form a stiff dough.

3 Turn the dough out onto a lightly floured work surface. Knead the dough until glossy and elastic, about 10 minutes.

4 Put the dough in a large, lightly oiled bowl. Turn the dough to coat with the oil and cover with a dish towel. Let rise until doubled in size, about 1 hour. Punch down the dough, then let rest for 10 minutes.

5 Shape the dough for a loaf pan (see page 53) and place in the pan, seam side down. Cover loosely with a dish towel. Proof until doubled in size, about 30 minutes.

6 Brush the top of the loaf with water and sprinkle with the oat flakes or rolled oats.

7 Bake in the preheated oven for 40 minutes. Turn the loaf out of the pan, and return it to the oven, bottom side up, for 5 minutes. Cool on a wire rack.

VARIATIONS

Sunflower and Honey Bread
• Make one quantity Multigrain Bread dough, replacing the ground and cooked multigrain cereals with 1 cup sunflower seeds and 2 tablespoons wheat germ. Add to the well as directed in step 2 and increase the amount of honey from 2 to 3 tablespoons.
• Continue as directed up to step 6. Sprinkle the loaf with sunflower seeds, instead of the oat flakes.
• Bake as directed in step 7.

Cracked Grain Bread
• Put ½ cup each cracked buckwheat, cracked wheat, and cracked rye in a bowl; pour boiling water over to cover. Let stand for 30 minutes until swollen, then drain.
• Make one quantity Multigrain Bread dough, replacing the multigrain cereals with the cracked grains and 2 tablespoons flaxseeds.
• Continue as directed up to step 6. Sprinkle the top of the loaf with 2 tablespoons sesame seeds, instead of the oat flakes or rolled oats.
• Bake as directed in step 7.

Multigrain Rolls
• Make one quantity Multigrain Bread dough to step 5.
• Divide it into eight equal pieces and shape into round rolls (see page 55).
• Place on a greased baking sheet; cover with a dish towel. Proof until doubled in size, about 40 minutes.
• Preheat the oven to 400°F. Use scissors to snip an "X" in each roll (see page 62). Top the rolls as directed in step 6, then bake for 30 minutes.

Rising
1 hour
(see pages 50–51)

Proofing
30 minutes
(see page 57)

Oven temperature
400°F

Baking
45 minutes
Steam optional
(see page 63)

Yield
1 loaf

Yeast alternative
1 cake (0.6oz) yeast
(see page 41)

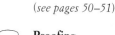

PANE CON POMODORI E CIPOLLE ROSSE

TOMATO AND RED ONION BREAD

This robustly flavored loaf originated in Tropea in the southern Italian region of Calabria, where tomatoes and onions flourish, and strong, peppery dishes are favored. Ripe, full-flavored tomatoes are essential to the success of this recipe. Choose firm, red tomatoes or leave them stem side down on a window sill to ripen. Store ripe tomatoes in a dark, cool place. Never refrigerate tomatoes—cold temperatures make the flesh pulpy and destroy the tomato flavor.

PANE CON POMODORI E CIPOLLE ROSSE

INGREDIENTS

3½ tsp dry yeast
⅔ cup water
4 cups bread flour
2 tsp salt
1lb ripe tomatoes
1 tbsp olive oil
2 red onions, halved and finely sliced
3 tsp chopped fresh oregano
1 tsp crushed red pepper flakes

1 Sprinkle the yeast into the water in a bowl. Let stand for 5 minutes; stir to dissolve. Mix the flour and salt in a large bowl. Make a well in the center of the flour and pour in the dissolved yeast.

2 Use a wooden spoon to draw enough of the flour into the dissolved yeast to form a thick paste. Cover the bowl with a dish towel and let "sponge" until frothy and risen, about 1 hour.

3 To skin the tomatoes, immerse them in boiling water for 1 minute. Score the skin with a knife and peel it away. Cut the tomatoes in half, remove the cores, scoop out the seeds, and roughly chop the flesh. Reserve the flesh only.

4 Heat the olive oil in a pan, then add the tomatoes, sliced onions, oregano, and red pepper flakes. Cover the pan and cook gently for 10 minutes. Transfer the tomato mixture to a bowl and let cool.

5 Stir the cooled tomato mixture into the fermented sponge. Mix in the flour to make a soft, sticky dough. The moisture content of the tomatoes will affect the consistency. Add flour if the dough is too wet.

6 Turn the dough out onto a lightly floured work surface. Knead until silky and supple, about 10 minutes.

7 Put the dough in a lightly oiled bowl and cover with a dish towel. Let rise until doubled in size, about 1 hour. Punch down and chafe, 5 minutes (see page 51), then let rest for about 10 minutes.

8 Shape the dough into a round loaf (see page 54). Place on an oiled baking sheet and cover with a dish towel. Proof until doubled in size, about 35–45 minutes.

9 Bake in the preheated oven for 45 minutes, until golden and hollow sounding when tapped underneath. Cool on a wire rack.

To begin
Sponge method
Time: 1 hour
(see page 44)

Rising
1 hour
(see pages 50–51)

Proofing
35–45 minutes
(see page 57)

Oven temperature
400°F

Baking
45 minutes
Steam optional
(see page 63)

Yield
1 loaf

Yeast alternative
1¾ cakes
(0.6oz-sized) yeast
(see page 41)

DARK CHOCOLATE BREAD

A portion of the flour is replaced with cocoa to produce this deeply savory, bittersweet bread. This chocolate bread is the perfect accompaniment to a rich winter stew of beef or game.

INGREDIENTS

2 tsp dry yeast

1⅔ cups water

4 tbsp sugar

2⅔ cups bread flour

1¼ cups cocoa powder

1½ tsp salt

1 Sprinkle the yeast into ½ cup of the water in a bowl. Let stand for 5 minutes, then add the sugar; stir to dissolve. Sift the flour, cocoa, and salt together into a large bowl. Make a well in the center and pour in the dissolved yeast.

2 Pour about half of the remaining water into the well. Mix in the flour from the sides of the well. Stir in the reserved water, as needed, to form a stiff dough.

3 Turn the dough out onto a lightly floured work surface. Knead until smooth, silky, and elastic, about 10 minutes.

4 Put the dough in a clean bowl; cover with a dish towel. Let rise until doubled in size, about 1 hour. Punch down the dough, then let rest for 10 minutes.

5 Shape the dough into a round loaf (*see page 54*). Place on a lightly floured baking sheet and cover with a dish towel. Proof until doubled in size, about 45 minutes.

6 Dust the loaf with cocoa powder. Use a series of slashes, ½ inch deep, across the top of the loaf (*see page 62*) to make a pattern (*see left*). Bake in the preheated oven for 45 minutes, until hollow sounding when tapped underneath. Cool on a wire rack.

 Rising
1 hour
(*see pages 50–51*)

 Proofing
45 minutes
(*see page 57*)

 Oven temperature
425°F

 Baking
45 minutes
Steam optional
(*see page 63*)

 Yield
1 loaf

 Yeast alternative
1 cake (0.6oz) yeast
(*see page 41*)

SOUTH AFRICAN SEED BREAD

This seed-packed, super-healthy bread with a nutty, cakey crumb and a soft, golden crust is unique to South Africa. It is a relatively quick yeast bread to make since it requires no kneading and only one rise after the dough has been shaped.

INGREDIENTS

unsalted butter, melted, to grease pan

3 tsp dry yeast

1⅔ cups water

4 tsp honey

3 cups whole-wheat flour

1 cup bread flour

3 tbsp each sesame seeds, sunflower seeds, flaxseeds, poppy seeds, chopped mixed nuts

1½ tsp salt

1 tbsp milk

1 Grease an 8 x 4 x 2½-inch loaf pan with the butter. Sprinkle the yeast into 1¼ cups of the water in a bowl; add the honey. Let stand for 5 minutes; stir to dissolve. Mix the flours, seeds, nuts, and salt in a bowl.

2 Make a well in the center of the flour mixture and pour in the dissolved yeast. Mix in the flour from the sides of the well. Stir in the remaining water, as needed, to form a soft, sticky dough that just begins to leave the sides of the bowl clean.

3 Spoon the dough into the greased pan using the back of the spoon to smooth it level. Proof until the dough has risen just above the rim of the pan, about 1 hour.

4 Bake in the preheated oven for 30 minutes, then reduce the oven to 350°F and bake for 30 minutes. The top of the bread will remain flat. Turn out onto a wire rack to cool. Immediately brush the top and sides of the loaf with milk.

 Proofing
1 hour
(*see page 57*)

 Oven temperature
400°F

 Baking
1 hour

 Yield
1 loaf

 Yeast alternative
1½ cakes
(0.6oz-sized) yeast
(*see page 41*)

HUNGARIAN POTATO BREAD

Adapted from George Lang's book Cuisine of Hungary, this unusual bread is truly worth making. We love its moist, springy crumb and earthy, subtly spiced flavor. During proofing, the loaf will not rise as much as most doughs because of the denseness of the potatoes. However, once the bread is placed in a hot oven, the moisture in the potatoes will cause the loaf to expand dramatically.

INGREDIENTS

2 medium-size floury potatoes, peeled (about 1lb)

2 tsp dry yeast

2¼ cups bread flour

1½ tsp salt

½ tsp caraway seeds

1 Boil the potatoes until soft, then drain, reserving ¾ cup of the cooking water. Mash the potatoes thoroughly, pushing them through a sieve or food mill to form 2¼ cups of smooth and fluffy mashed potatoes. Let the potatoes and cooking water cool until lukewarm.

2 Sprinkle the yeast into ½ cup plus 2 tablespoons of the water in a bowl. Let stand for 5 minutes; stir to dissolve. Put the flour in a large bowl. Make a well in the center and pour in the dissolved yeast.

3 Use a wooden spoon to draw enough of the flour into the dissolved yeast to form a soft paste. Cover the bowl with a dish towel and let "sponge" until frothy and slightly risen, about 20 minutes.

4 Add the mashed potatoes, salt, and caraway seeds to the well.

Mix in the flour thoroughly with a wooden spoon, adding the reserved cooking water, as needed, to form a soft, moist dough.

5 Turn the dough out onto a lightly floured work surface. Knead until smooth, shiny, and soft, about 10 minutes.

6 Put the dough in a clean bowl and cover with a dish towel. Let rise until doubled in size, about 2 hours. Punch down, then let rest for 10 minutes.

7 Shape the dough into a smooth, round loaf (see page 54). Place on a lightly floured baking sheet and cover with a dish towel. Proof until the dough is well risen and springs back slowly when gently pressed with a finger, about 30 minutes.

8 Dust the loaf with flour. Cut three parallel slashes, ½ inch deep, across the top, then three slashes in the opposite direction to make a crisscross pattern (see page 62).

9 Bake in the preheated oven for 1 hour, until crusty and hollow sounding when tapped underneath. Cool on a wire rack.

 To begin
Sponge method
Time: 20 minutes
(see page 44)

 Rising
2 hours
(see pages 50–51)

 Proofing
30 minutes
(see page 57)

 Oven temperature
425°F

 Baking
1 hour
Steam optional
(see page 63)

 Yield
1 loaf

 Yeast alternative
1 cake (0.6oz) yeast
(see page 41)

FOCACCIA FARCITA
FILLED ITALIAN HEARTH BREAD

This Italian bread got its name from the Latin word focus, which means "hearth." The embers of the hearth are where Focaccia was traditionally baked. Fillings and toppings for Focaccia are very much a movable feast. Generally speaking, Italian-style ingredients such as roasted peppers, sun-dried tomatoes, salty olives, capers, fragrant fresh herbs, grilled eggplants, or vine-ripened plum tomatoes will complement this bread dough to perfection. Keep in mind that any topping or filling must be cooked in the same time that it takes the bread to bake. Therefore, vegetables have to be chopped or sliced and partially cooked by roasting or parboiling before they can be used.

INGREDIENTS

2 tsp dry yeast

1¼ cups water

3¼ cups bread flour

1½ tsp salt

3 tbsp olive oil

for the filling and topping

½ cup crumbled Gorgonzola

7oz mozzarella, sliced

1 handful of basil leaves

½ tsp coarse salt

2 tbsp fresh rosemary leaves

4 tbsp olive oil

1 Sprinkle the yeast into 1 cup of the water in a bowl. Let stand for 5 minutes; stir to dissolve. Mix the flour and salt in a large bowl. Make a well in the center of the flour and pour in the dissolved yeast and the oil.

2 Mix in the flour. Stir in the remaining water to form a soft, sticky dough. Add more water, 1 tablespoon at a time, if needed.

3 Turn the dough out onto a lightly floured work surface. Knead until smooth, silky, and elastic, about 10 minutes.

4 Put the dough in an oiled bowl and cover with a dish towel. Let rise until doubled in size, about 1½–2 hours. Punch down and divide the dough into two equal pieces. Chafe for 5 minutes (see page 51), then let rest for 10 minutes.

5 **To make the filling** Roll out each piece of dough into a 9½-inch round. Place one round on an oiled baking sheet. Arrange the two cheeses and basil over the top, then seal in the filling using the second round (see right).

6 Cover the dough loosely with a dish towel. Proof until doubled in size, about 30 minutes.

7 Use your fingertips to gently press into the surface of the dough to form dimples about ½ inch deep. Sprinkle with the coarse salt, rosemary leaves, and 1 tablespoon of the olive oil.

8 Bake in the preheated oven for 30–45 minutes, until golden. Drizzle immediately with the remaining olive oil, and serve warm.

VARIATION
Focaccia with Tomato, Arugula, and Mozzarella
• Preheat the oven to 400°F. Place 1lb cherry tomatoes on a baking sheet and sprinkle with 1 tablespoon olive oil, and season with salt and pepper. Bake for 20 minutes.
• Cut 5oz mozzarella into cherry tomato-size pieces. Wash and dry 6½ cups arugula leaves.
• Make one quantity Focaccia Farcita dough, replacing the filling in step 5 with the tomatoes, mozzarella, and arugula.
• Continue as directed in steps 6–8.

 Rising
1½–2 hours
(see pages 50–51)

 Proofing
30 minutes
(see page 57)

 Oven temperature
400°F

 Baking
30–45 minutes
Steam optional
(see page 63)

 Yield
1 loaf

Yeast alternative
1 cake (0.6oz) yeast
(see page 41)

SEALING IN THE FILLING

To seal the filling, place the second round of dough over the top of the filling. Seal the edges of the dough by gently pinching them together with your fingers.

STROMBOLI

ROLLED HEARTH BREAD FILLED WITH SMOKED MOZZARELLA AND BASIL

Named after the volcanic island of Stromboli, located off the coast of Sicily, this bread is filled with a delicious combination of smoked and plain mozzarella. The cheeses erupt from the holes pierced in the rolled Focaccia dough during baking. Serve it still warm from the oven for the most enjoyment.

INGREDIENTS

2 tsp dry yeast

1¼ cups water

3¾ cups bread flour

1½ tsp salt

3 tbsp olive oil

for the filling and topping

1½ cups chopped mozzarella

1½ cups chopped smoked mozzarella

1 garlic clove, peeled and chopped

1 handful of fresh basil leaves

3 tbsp olive oil

1 tsp coarse salt

3 sprigs rosemary, stems removed

1 tsp pepper

1 Sprinkle the yeast into 1 cup of the water in a bowl. Let stand for 5 minutes; stir to dissolve.

2 Mix the flour and salt in a large bowl. Make a well in the center and pour in the dissolved yeast and the oil. Mix in the flour from the sides of the well. Stir in the reserved water, as needed, to form a soft, sticky dough.

3 Turn the dough out onto a lightly floured work surface. Knead until smooth, silky, and elastic, about 10 minutes.

4 Put the dough in a clean, oiled bowl and cover with a dish towel. Let rise until doubled in size, 1½–2 hours. Punch down and chafe for 5 minutes (see page 51), then let rest for 10 minutes.

5 Shape the dough into a 14-inch x 8-inch rectangle. Cover with a dish towel and let rest for 10 minutes.

6 **To make the filling and topping** Spread the cheeses, garlic, and basil leaves evenly over the dough. Roll the dough like a Swiss roll, starting at one of the shorter sides, but without rolling too tightly.

7 Place on an oiled baking sheet. Use a skewer or a carving fork to pierce several holes through the dough to the baking sheet. Sprinkle with 1 tablespoon of the olive oil, salt, rosemary leaves, and pepper.

8 Bake in the preheated oven for 1 hour, until golden. Cool slightly, then drizzle with the remaining olive oil.

Rising
1½–2 hours
(see pages 50–51)

Oven temperature
400°F

Baking
1 hour
Steam optional
(see page 63)

Yield
1 loaf

Yeast alternative
1 cake (0.6oz) yeast
(see page 41)

FOCACCIA CON OLIVE
HEARTH BREAD WITH OLIVES

Focaccia *originated in Genoa, but numerous variations on the classic salt and olive oil Genoese hearth bread are found all over Liguria. This recipe calls for the famous olives, olive oil, and white wine of the region – the wine, in particular, adds another flavor dimension. This bread is best eaten while still warm.*

INGREDIENTS

2 tsp dry yeast

¾ cup water

3¾ cups bread flour

1½ tsp salt

⅓ cup olive oil,
plus additional olive oil to finish

⅓ cup dry white wine

1½ cups pitted black olives,
coarsely chopped

2 tbsp fresh thyme leaves

1 tbsp chopped fresh oregano

1 Sprinkle the yeast into ½ cup of the water in a bowl. Let stand for 5 minutes; stir to dissolve. Mix the flour and salt in a large bowl. Make a well in the center and pour in the dissolved yeast.

2 Use a wooden spoon to draw enough of the flour into the dissolved yeast to form a soft paste. Cover the bowl with a dish towel and let "sponge" until frothy and risen, about 20 minutes.

3 Add the olive oil and the white wine to the well. Mix in the flour. Stir in the remaining water, as needed, to form a soft, sticky dough.

4 Turn the dough out onto a lightly floured work surface. Knead until smooth and elastic, about 10 minutes. Work ¾ cup of the olives and 1 tablespoon of the thyme into the dough toward the end of kneading (*see page 99*).

5 Put the dough in an oiled bowl and cover with a dish towel. Let rise until doubled in size, 1½–2 hours. Punch down and chafe for 5 minutes (*see page 51*), then let rest for 10 minutes.

6 Roll out the dough on a lightly floured work surface to form a 9½-inch round, ½ inch thick. Place on an oiled baking sheet and cover with a dish towel. Proof until doubled in size, about 1 hour.

7 Use your fingertips to press into the surface of the dough to form dimples about ½ inch deep. Sprinkle with the oregano and the remaining olives and thyme.

8 Bake in the preheated oven for 30 minutes, until golden brown and hollow sounding when tapped underneath. Sprinkle with additional oil immediately. Cool on a wire rack.

VARIATION
Focaccia alla Salvia
(Italian Hearth Bread with Sage)
• Make one quantity Focaccia con Olive dough up to step 3.
• Add 20 chopped fresh sage leaves to the sponge with the oil and the wine in step 3. Mix in the flour and stir in the water as directed.
• Continue as directed in steps 4–6.
• Dimple the dough as directed in step 7 and replace the olives, thyme, and oregano with 1½ teaspoons coarse salt, 2 tablespoons olive oil, and ten fresh sage leaves.
• Bake as directed in step 8.

To begin
Sponge method
Time: 20 minutes
(*see page 44*)

Rising
1½–2 hours
(*see pages 50–51*)

Proofing
1 hour
(*see page 57*)

Oven temperature
400°F

Baking
30 minutes
Steam optional
(*see page 63*)

Yield
1 loaf

Yeast alternative
1 cake (0.6oz) yeast
(*see page 41*)

FOCACCIA ALLA SALVIA

SCHIACCIATA CON LE CIPOLLE ROSSE E FORMAGGIO

SCHIACCIATA WITH ROASTED RED ONIONS AND CHEESE

Schiacciata, *which translates as "squashed" or "flattened," is the word Florentines use to describe their version of Genoese* Focaccia. *Sweet roasted red onions and sharp Gruyère cheese make a scrumptious topping for this light, airy* Focaccia *dough.*

INGREDIENTS

for the starter

½ tsp dry yeast

⅔ cup water

1 cup bread flour

for the dough

1½ tsp dry yeast

1 cup plus 2 tbsp water

2¼ cups bread flour

1½ tsp salt

3 tbsp olive oil

for the topping

2 cups grated Gruyère

3 red onions, each cut into 8 wedges

2 tsp fresh thyme leaves

4 tbsp olive oil

1 tsp coarse salt

1 **To make the starter** Sprinkle the yeast into the water. Let stand for 5 minutes; stir to dissolve. Add the flour and mix to form a thick batter. Cover with a dish towel and ferment at room temperature for at least 12 and up to 36 hours, until it forms a loose, bubbling batter.

2 **To make the dough** Sprinkle the yeast into ½ cup of the water. Let stand for 5 minutes; stir to dissolve. Mix the flour and the salt in a large bowl. Make a well in the center, pour in the dissolved yeast and olive oil, then add the starter.

3 Mix in the flour. Stir in the remaining water, as needed, to form a soft, sticky dough. Add extra water, 1 tablespoon at a time, if necessary.

4 Turn out onto a lightly floured work surface. Knead the dough until smooth, silky, and elastic, about 10 minutes.

5 Put the dough in a clean, lightly oiled bowl and cover with a dish towel. Let rise until doubled in size, 1½–2 hours. Punch down and chafe for 5 minutes (*see page 51*), then let rest, about 10 minutes.

6 Roll out the dough on a lightly floured work surface to form a round, 9½ inches in diameter.

7 Place the dough on a lightly oiled baking sheet and cover with a dish towel. Proof until doubled in size, about 30 minutes.

8 **To make the topping** Use your fingertips to gently press into the dough to make dimples about ½ inch deep. Scatter an even layer of Gruyère and onion wedges on top of the dough, then sprinkle with the thyme, oil, and salt.

9 Bake in the preheated oven for 30 minutes, until puffed and the topping is crisp. Cool slightly on a wire rack. Cut into wedges and serve while still warm. It is also good at room temperature.

To begin
Starter
Time: 12–36 hours
(*see page 44*)

Rising
1½–2 hours
(*see pages 50–51*)

Proofing
30 minutes
(*see page 57*)

Oven temperature
400°F

Baking
30 minutes
Steam optional
(*see page 63*)

Yield
1 loaf

Yeast alternative
For the starter:
⅛ of a cake
(0.6oz-sized) yeast
For the dough:
¾ of a cake
(0.6oz-sized) yeast
(*see page 41*)

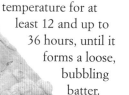

SCHIACCIATA CON L'UVA
SCHIACCIATA WITH BLACK GRAPES AND WINE-SOAKED RAISINS

This Schiacciata is traditionally made in Tuscany at grape harvest time with the Sangiovese grapes that are used to make Chianti Classico wines. The raisins inside the dough represent the last season's grapes, while the new season's grapes are used to adorn the top.

INGREDIENTS
for the starter

1 *quantity starter* (see Schiacciata con le Cipolle Rosse e Formaggio, page 108)

for the dough

3 tbsp sugar

1 *quantity dough* (see Schiacciata con le Cipolle Rosse e Formaggio, page 108)

for the filling and topping

1¼ packed cup raisins

1 glass of Vin Santo
or another sweet dessert wine

1lb seedless black grapes

3 tbsp light brown granulated sugar

1 tsp fennel seeds

1 To make the starter and dough Make the starter and dough as directed for Schiacciata con le Cipolle Rosse e Formaggio (*see page 108*), up to step 5. Add the sugar to the flour and salt in step 2.

2 Put the dough in a lightly oiled bowl and cover with a dish towel. Let rise until doubled in size, 1½–2 hours. Punch down and chafe for 5 minutes (*see page 51*), then let rest, about 10 minutes.

3 Divide the dough into two equal pieces. Roll out each piece of dough on a lightly floured surface to form two 9½-inch rounds. Place one round on a lightly oiled baking sheet.

4 Marinate the raisins in the wine for at least 2 hours or, preferably, overnight. Drain them thoroughly and reserve the leftover wine as a special treat for the baker to drink.

5 To make the filling Spread the raisins evenly over the first dough round. Put the second round on top and pinch the edges together, then cover with a dish towel. Proof until doubled in size, about 30 minutes.

6 Cover the dough evenly with the grapes, lightly pressing them into the dough, and sprinkle the light brown granulated sugar and fennel seeds on the top.

7 Bake in the preheated oven for 45 minutes, until the crust is golden and the grapes are lightly browned. Cool slightly on a wire rack.

To begin
Starter
Time: 12–36 hours
(*see page 44*)

Rising
1½–2 hours
(*see pages 50–51*)

Proofing
30 minutes
(*see page 57*)

Oven temperature
400°F

Baking
45 minutes
Steam optional
(*see page 63*)

Yield
1 loaf

Yeast alternative
For the starter:
⅛ of a cake
(0.6oz-sized) yeast
For the dough:
¾ of a cake
(0.6oz-sized) yeast
(*see page 41*)

ENRICHED BREADS

THE ADDITION OF ONE OR MORE ENRICHING INGREDIENTS—SUCH AS BUTTER, OIL, OR EGGS—RESULTS IN A BREAD WITH A SOFT, TENDER CRUMB THAT BECOMES MORE CAKELIKE IN DIRECT PROPORTION TO THE QUANTITIES OF THE ENRICHMENTS ADDED. THE MOISTURE IN THESE INGREDIENTS MAKES THE DOUGH SOFT AND OFTEN DIFFICULT TO HANDLE. THE FAT IN THEM COATS THE GLUTEN STRANDS IN THE DOUGH AND CREATES A BARRIER BETWEEN THE FLOUR AND THE YEAST. THIS LENGTHENS THE RISING TIMES SO MUCH THAT IN BREADS LIKE BRIOCHE, THE ENRICHMENTS ARE ADDED AFTER THE INITIAL RISING. THE RECIPES IN THIS SECTION MAY REQUIRE SOME NEW SKILLS AND A BIT MORE CONFIDENCE AND TIME THAN PREVIOUS RECIPES, BUT THEY ARE WORTH IT.

LEFT **AN INDIVIDUAL BRIOCHE AND THE LARGER BRIOCHE À TÊTE**

BRIOCHE

Egg-and-butter-enriched Brioche *dough is formed into a variety of shapes, but perhaps the classic and most characteristic is that of the small* Brioche Parisienne, *with its distinctive topknot and scalloped underside. Perhaps best enjoyed at breakfast with raspberry preserves and a bowl of steaming* café au lait, Brioche *boasts a culinary status that far outstrips that of the breakfast table.* Brioche *dough is favored above other doughs and pastries in some celebrated classic dishes, most notably Beef Wellington.*

INGREDIENTS

2½ tsp dry yeast

2 tbsp water

2¼ cups bread flour

2 tbsp sugar

1½ tsp salt

5 medium eggs, beaten

1 tbsp melted butter, to brush bowl

12 tbsp unsalted butter, softened, plus extra to brush molds

egg glaze, made with 1 egg yolk and 1 tbsp water (see page 58)

1 Sprinkle the yeast into the water in a bowl. Let stand for 5 minutes; stir to dissolve. Mix the flour, sugar, and salt in a large bowl.

2 Make a well in the center and add the dissolved yeast and beaten eggs (*see below, left*). Mix in the flour to form a soft, moist but manageable dough.

3 Turn the dough out onto a lightly floured work surface. Knead until elastic, about 10 minutes.

4 Grease a large bowl with the melted butter. Place the dough in the bowl; turn it to coat evenly. Cover with a dish towel and let rise until doubled in size, about 1–1½ hours. Punch down, then let rest for 10 minutes.

5 Use your hand to incorporate the softened butter into the dough (*see below, right*).

6 Turn out onto a lightly floured work surface. Knead until the butter is distributed throughout, 5 minutes, then rest for 5 minutes more. Grease ten brioche molds, each about 3½ inches in diameter and 2 inches deep, with softened butter (*see opposite, left*).

7 Divide the dough into ten pieces. Pinch off about a quarter of each piece. Use cupped hands to roll both the large and small pieces of dough into smooth balls (*see page 55*). Place one of the large balls into each of the prepared brioche molds.

8 Use your forefinger to make an indentation in the center of the large ball, then add the small ball (*see opposite, right*). Repeat this step with the remaining balls of dough.

9 Cover the molds with a dish towel and proof until the dough has doubled in size, 30 minutes.

10 Brush the tops of the dough with the egg glaze. Place the molds on a baking sheet. Bake in the preheated oven for 15–20 minutes, until glossy and golden. Turn out and cool on a wire rack.

Rising
1–1½ hours
(*see pages 50–51*)

Proofing
30 minutes
(*see page 57*)

Oven temperature
425°F

Baking
15–20 minutes

Yield
10 small Brioche

Yeast alternative
1¼ cakes
(0.6oz-sized) yeast
(*see page 41*)

ADDING ENRICHMENTS TO DOUGH

In step 2, add beaten eggs directly to the flour well along with the dissolved yeast. Mix in the flour to form a soft, moist but manageable dough.

In step 5, use your hand to squeeze the softened butter into the dough until evenly distributed throughout. Continue as directed in step 6.

PREPARING THE MOLD AND DOUGH FOR BAKING

In step 6, grease the mold with softened butter, then place it in the refrigerator until the butter is hard. Once the butter has formed a hardened shell, grease the mold a second time with more softened butter.

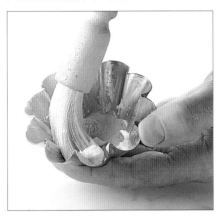

In step 8, use your forefinger to make a slight indentation in the center of each large ball. Brush the indentation with egg glaze. Place a smaller ball on top to make a topknot. Repeat with the remaining dough balls and molds.

VARIATIONS
Brioche à Tête
(Large Brioche with a Topknot)
• Make one quantity Brioche dough up to step 7, replacing the ten small molds in step 6 with a buttered brioche mold, 7 inches in diameter and 6 inches deep.
• Pinch off a third of the dough. Shape the large piece of dough into a round loaf (*see page 54*). Use cupped hands to roll the small piece into a round roll (*see page 55*).
• Put the large ball, seam side down, in the brioche mold. Make an indentation, then add the small ball.
• Cover and proof until the dough fills the mold, about 45 minutes. Preheat the oven to 425°F.
• Brush the dough with the egg glaze. Bake for 35–45 minutes, until glossy and golden. Turn out of the brioche mold onto a wire rack to cool.

Brioche Nanterre
(Brioche from Nanterre)
• Make one quantity Brioche dough up to step 7, replacing the molds in step 6 with a buttered 9 x 5 x 3-inch loaf pan.
• Divide the dough into eight pieces. Use cupped hands to roll each piece into a ball (*see page 55*).
• Put the eight rolls of dough in the prepared loaf pan, placing them four to a row down each side of the pan.
• Cover with a dish towel and proof until the dough fills the pan, about 45 minutes. Preheat the oven to 400°F.

• Brush with the egg glaze. Bake for 35 minutes, until shiny, golden, and hollow sounding when tapped. Turn out of the loaf pan to cool.

Pain Amuse-gueule
(Flavored Brioche)
• Make one quantity Brioche dough up to step 7, adding 2 cups diced Gruyère, 1 tablespoon each dried *herbes de Provence*, dried mint, and dried oregano, and 1 teaspoon each caraway seeds, coriander seeds, and fennel seeds to the dough with the softened butter in step 5.
• Replace the molds with a buttered 9 x 5 x 3-inch loaf pan in step 6. Shape the dough for a pan loaf (*see page 53*).
• Put the dough in the prepared pan. Cover with a dish towel and proof until the dough rises to ¼ inch below the top of the pan, about 45 minutes. Preheat the oven to 400°F.
• Brush with the egg glaze and sprinkle with an additional 2 tablespoons grated Gruyère.
• Bake for 35 minutes, until golden and hollow sounding when tapped underneath. Turn out of the pan onto a wire rack to cool.

— HANDY TIPS —
• *Use the best-quality butter and freshest eggs available to make the most flavorful* Brioche.

• *Be sure that the eggs are at room temperature and the butter has been left out of the refrigerator to soften before starting.*

• *It is important to always use softened, not melted, butter to grease the brioche molds.*

• *Use leftover* Brioche *to make luxurious* Pain Perdu *or a scrumptious* Bread and Butter Pudding *(see pages 158–159).*

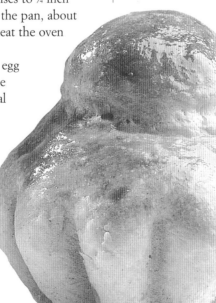

MANTOVANA
OLIVE OIL BREAD FROM MANTUA

This long loaf, with its delicate, crispy crust and fine crumb, takes its name, Mantovana, *from Mantua in Lombardy, Italy. The double rising produces a bread with a light, even texture. Be careful not to overrise the dough—it might collapse upon being placed in a hot oven; do not leave the dough for any longer than 40 minutes for its second rising. Serve with sliced Prociutto ham or country salami or other antipasti.*

INGREDIENTS

2 tsp dry yeast	
2½ cups water	
1½ cups whole-wheat flour	
3¾ cups bread flour	
2 tsp salt	
½ cup olive oil	

1 Sprinkle the yeast into 1⅔ cups of the water in a bowl. Let stand for 5 minutes; stir to dissolve. Mix the flours in a large bowl. Make a well in the center and pour in the dissolved yeast.

2 Use a wooden spoon to draw enough of the flour into the dissolved yeast to form a soft paste. Cover the bowl with a dish towel, then let "sponge" until frothy and risen, about 20 minutes.

3 Add the salt and oil to the sponge. Mix in the rest of the flour from the sides of the well. Stir in the remaining water, as needed, to form a very sticky dough.

4 Turn the dough out onto a floured work surface. Knead until smooth, about 10 minutes.

5 Put the dough in a clean, oiled bowl; cover with a dish towel. Let rise until doubled in size, about 50 minutes. Punch down, cover with a dish towel, and let rise until doubled in size, about 40 minutes.

6 Punch down and chafe for 10 minutes (*see page 51*), then let rest for 10 minutes.

7 Divide the dough into two pieces. Shape each piece into a long loaf (*see page 52*), about 10 inches in length. Place on a floured baking sheet and cover with a dish towel. Proof for 15 minutes.

8 Cut a lengthwise slash, ½ inch deep, down the center of each loaf (*see page 62*). Bake in the preheated oven for 45 minutes, until golden and hollow sounding when tapped underneath. Cool on a wire rack.

To begin
Sponge method
Time: 20 minutes
(*see page 44*)

Rising
1½ hours
(*see pages 50–51*)

Proofing
15 minutes
(*see page 57*)

Oven temperature
400°F

Baking
45 minutes

Yield
2 loaves

Yeast alternative
1 cake (0.6oz) yeast
(*see page 41*)

PANE DI RAMERINO
ROSEMARY RAISIN BREAD

Quite simply the best accompaniment to fresh goat cheese, Panmarino is a superlative breakfast bread, too. This bread recipe is a Florentine specialty that has been baked daily throughout Tuscany since the early 16th century. It is enriched with milk, olive oil, and eggs, ingredients that reflect its origins. Fresh rosemary and raisins made from the region's famous grapes abound in Tuscan cuisine, as do the figs and almonds that inspired this recipe's delicious variation.

INGREDIENTS

2 tsp dry yeast
½ cup water
3¼ cups bread flour
1½ tsp salt
2 tbsp powdered milk
1 tbsp fresh rosemary, chopped
1½ packed cups raisins
4 tbsp olive oil
4 eggs, beaten

1 Sprinkle the yeast into the water in a bowl. Let stand for 5 minutes; stir to dissolve. Mix the flour, salt, and powdered milk in a large mixing bowl. Make a well in the center and add the dissolved yeast and all the remaining ingredients.

2 Mix the flour into the yeast mixture to form a soft, sticky dough. Add extra flour, 1 tablespoon at a time, if the dough is too moist.

3 Turn the dough out onto a lightly floured work surface. Knead until silky, springy, and elastic, about 10 minutes.

4 Put the dough in a clean, oiled bowl and cover with a dish towel. Let rise until doubled in size, about 2 hours. Punch down and chafe for 5 minutes (*see page 51*), then let rest for 10 minutes.

5 Divide the dough into two pieces. Shape each into a round loaf (*see page 54*).

Place on two oiled baking sheets and cover with dish towels. Proof until doubled in size, about 1 hour. These loaves will spread and look slightly flat after rising, but they will rise up dramatically during the initial stages of baking.

6 Cut a slash, ½ inch deep, across the top of the loaf, then another in the opposite direction to make an "X" (*see page 62*).

7 Bake in the preheated oven for 45 minutes, until golden brown and hollow sounding when tapped underneath. Cool on a wire rack.

VARIATION
Pane ai Fichi con Mandorle (Fig Bread with Almonds)

• Make one quantity Panmarino dough up to step 7, replacing the rosemary with 1 cup whole almonds, toasted and chopped; the raisins with the same amount of finely chopped dried figs; and the olive oil with the same amount of orange juice. Preheat the oven to 400°F.

• Bake as directed in step 7. Dust the top with a generous amount of confectioners' sugar before serving.

Rising
2 hours
(*see pages 50–51*)

Proofing
1 hour
(*see page 57*)

Oven temperature
400°F

Baking
45 minutes

Yield
2 loaves

Yeast alternative
1 cake (0.6oz) yeast
(*see page 41*)

TORTA DI TESTA DI PROSCIUTTO E FORMAGGIO

GOLDEN CHEESE AND HAM BREAD

This lovely golden loaf, marbeled with savory morsels of ham and cheese, makes a perfect accompaniment—fresh, warm, or toasted—to a bowl of hot soup. It also makes a delicious base for the ultimate grilled cheese sandwich.

INGREDIENTS

2 tsp dry yeast

½ cup water

3¼ cups bread flour

1½ tsp salt

¼ tsp freshly ground black pepper

pinch of freshly grated nutmeg

8 tbsp unsalted butter, softened

4 eggs, beaten

5oz sliced prosciutto, chopped

1⅛ cups diced Emmental

oil, to grease baking sheet

1 Sprinkle the yeast into the water in a bowl. Let stand for 5 minutes; stir to dissolve. Mix the flour, salt, pepper, and nutmeg in a large bowl. Make a well in the center and add the dissolved yeast, butter, eggs, prosciutto, and cheese.

2 Mix the flour from the sides of the well into the dissolved yeast to form a soft, sticky dough.

3 Turn out onto a lightly floured work surface. Knead until silky and elastic, about 10 minutes.

4 Put the dough in a clean bowl and cover with a dish towel. Let rise until doubled in size, about 2 hours. Punch down, then let rest for 10 minutes.

5 Shape the dough into a round loaf (*see page 54*). Place on a lightly oiled baking sheet and cover with a dish towel. Proof until doubled in size, about 1 hour.

6 Bake in the preheated oven for 1½ hours, until golden brown. Cool on a wire rack.

Rising
2 hours
(*see pages 50–51*)

Proofing
1 hour
(*see page 57*)

Oven temperature
350°F

Baking
1½ hours

Yield
1 loaf

Yeast alternative
1 cake (0.6oz) yeast
(*see page 41*)

TORTA DI TESTA DI PROSCIUTTO E FORMAGGIO

ZOPF
SWISS BRAIDED LOAF

This shiny, golden milk loaf is made throughout Switzerland but is said to have originated in the Emmental region, where it is called Zupfe. The bread, enriched with the sweet butter and creamy milk of the region, then braided and baked to a glossy gold, is a traditional part of the annual thanksgiving meal in honor of the Emmentaler harvest. It is also very popular breakfast fare all over Switzerland, especially on New Year's Day.

INGREDIENTS

2 tsp dry yeast

1¼ cups milk

3¼ cups bread flour

1½ tsp salt

4 tbsp unsalted butter, softened and creamed, plus extra to grease baking sheet

1 tsp sugar

2 tbsp kirsch or brandy

egg glaze, made with 1 egg yolk and 1 tbsp milk (see page 58)

1 Sprinkle the yeast into ½ cup of the milk in a bowl. Let stand for 5 minutes; stir to dissolve. Put the flour in a large bowl. Make a well in the center and pour in the dissolved yeast.

2 Use a wooden spoon to draw enough of the flour into the dissolved yeast to form a soft paste. Cover the bowl with a dish towel, then let "sponge" until frothy and risen, about 20 minutes.

3 Pour about half of the remaining milk into the well. Mix in the flour, salt, butter, sugar, and kirsch or brandy. Stir in the reserved milk, as needed, to form a soft, moist dough.

4 Turn the dough out onto a lightly floured work surface.

Knead until smooth, shiny, and elastic, about 10 minutes.

5 Put the dough in a clean bowl and cover with a dish towel. Let rise until doubled in size, about 1½–2 hours. Punch down, then let rest for 10 minutes.

6 Divide the dough into three pieces. Roll out each piece to form a 16-inch-long rope and make a braided loaf (*see page 57*).

7 Place on a buttered baking sheet and cover with a dish towel. Proof until doubled in size, about 35–45 minutes. Brush the top of the loaf with the egg glaze.

8 Bake in the preheated oven for 40 minutes, until golden brown and hollow sounding when tapped underneath. Cool on a wire rack.

VARIATION
Pain Viennois (Vienna Bread)
• Make one quantity Zopf dough up to step 5, excluding the sugar and kirsch added in step 3.
• Divide the dough into two equal pieces, then shape each piece into an oval loaf (*see page 55*).
• Place on a buttered baking sheet and cover with a dish towel.
• Proof until doubled in size, about 1½–2 hours. Preheat the oven to 350°F.
• Brush with the egg glaze. Cut ten diagonal slashes, about ¼ inch deep, along the length of each loaf (*see page 62*). Bake for 35–45 minutes. Cool on a wire rack.

 To begin
Sponge method
Time: 20 minutes
(*see page 44*)

 Rising
1½–2 hours
(*see pages 50–51*)

 Proofing
35–45 minutes
(*see page 57*)

 Oven temperature
350°F

 Baking
40 minutes

 Yield
1 loaf

 Yeast alternative
1 cake (0.6oz) yeast
(*see page 41*)

ZOPF

117

PARKER HOUSE ROLLS

The Parker House Roll originated at the Parker House, a hotel in Boston. The butter-and-egg-enriched dough is cut into small rectangles, brushed with melted butter, folded in half, and baked until soft and golden brown. Serve these dangerously delicious rolls warm; cool them on a wire rack for 10 minutes, and then wrap them in a clean cloth to keep them warm.

INGREDIENTS

2½ tsp dry yeast

1 cup milk

4 tbsp unsalted butter, melted

2 tbsp sugar

2 eggs, beaten

4¼ cups bread flour

2 tsp salt

2 tbsp melted butter to glaze, plus extra to grease bowl and baking sheet

1 Sprinkle the yeast into ½ cup of the milk in a bowl. Let stand for 5 minutes; stir to dissolve. Warm the remaining milk in a saucepan with the butter and sugar. Stir until the butter has melted. Cool until lukewarm, then beat in the eggs until evenly combined.

2 Mix the flour and salt in a large bowl. Make a well in the center and pour in the dissolved yeast and the butter mixture. Mix in the flour to form a soft, sticky dough.

3 Turn the dough out onto a floured work surface. Knead until smooth, shiny, and elastic, about 10 minutes.

Knead in extra flour, 1 tablespoon at a time, if the dough is too sticky. Resist adding too much flour, as the dough should not be dry, but soft.

4 Put the dough in a buttered bowl and cover with a dish towel. Let rise until doubled in size, 1–1½ hours. Punch down, then let rest for 10 minutes.

5 Divide the dough into two pieces. Roll out each piece to form an 8 x 16-inch rectangle. Cut each rectangle lengthwise into four strips, each 2 inches wide. Cut each strip into four rectangles, each 4 inches long. Brush half of each rectangle with melted butter, then fold in half, leaving a ½-inch flap.

6 Place the rolls on a buttered baking sheet so that each roll overlaps slightly with the one next to it; cover with a dish towel. Proof until doubled in size, about 30 minutes.

7 Brush the tops of the rolls with melted butter. Bake in the preheated oven for 15–20 minutes, until golden and hollow sounding when tapped underneath. Cool on a wire rack.

 Rising
1–1½ hours
(see pages 50–51)

 Proofing
30 minutes
(see page 57)

 Oven temperature
425°F

 Baking
15–20 minutes

 Yield
16 rolls

 Yeast alternative
1¼ cakes
(0.6oz-sized) yeast
(see page 41)

PARKER HOUSE ROLLS

SHAPING A SNAIL ROLL

Roll each piece of dough into a 12-inch rope. Form each rope into a coil, tucking the end underneath.

VARIATIONS

Soft Dinner Rolls

• Make one quantity Parker House Rolls dough up to step 5.
• Divide the dough into 16 pieces. Shape each piece of dough into a round roll (see page 55).
• Arrange the rolls 2 inches apart on two buttered baking sheets. Cover with a dish towel and proof until doubled in size, 30 minutes.
• Brush each roll with an egg glaze, made with 1 egg yolk and 1 tablespoon milk. Preheat the oven to 425°F.
• Bake for 15–20 minutes, until golden. Cool on a wire rack.

Snail Rolls

• Make one quantity Parker House Rolls dough up to step 5.
• Divide the dough into 16 pieces. Roll each piece of dough into a 12-inch rope and form into a coil, tucking under the end.
• Place on two buttered baking sheets and proof as instructed for Soft Dinner Rolls. Preheat the oven to 425°F.
• Top the rolls as you prefer (see pages 58–61). Bake for 15–20 minutes, until golden. Cool on a wire rack.

Baker's Knot Rolls

• Make one quantity Parker House Rolls dough up to step 5.
• Divide the dough into 16 pieces. Roll each

piece into a 12-inch rope, then shape into a figure eight and tuck the ends through the holes.
• Place on two buttered baking sheets and proof as instructed for Soft Dinner Rolls. Preheat the oven to 425°F.
• Glaze and top the rolls as you prefer (see pages 58–61). Bake for 15–20 minutes. Cool on a wire rack.

Bow Knot Rolls

• Make one quantity Parker House Rolls dough up to step 5.
• Divide into 16 pieces. Shape each piece into a knot roll (see page 55).
• Place on two buttered baking sheets and proof as instructed for Soft Dinner Rolls. Preheat the oven to 425°F.
• Glaze and top the rolls as you prefer (see pages 58–61). Bake for 15–20 minutes. Cool on a wire rack.

Cloverleaf Rolls

• Make one quantity Parker House Rolls dough up to step 5.
• Divide into 16 pieces. Divide each piece into three even portions. Shape each piece into a round roll (see page 55). Place three balls in each buttered cup of a muffin tin.
• Proof until doubled in size, about 30 minutes. Preheat the oven to 425°F.
• Glaze and top the rolls as you prefer (see pages 58–61). Bake for 15–20 minutes. Cool on a wire rack.

Twist Rolls

• Make one quantity Parker House Rolls dough up to step 5.
• Divide the dough into 16 pieces. Roll each piece of dough into a 12-inch rope, fold in half, and twist; pinch the ends to seal.
• Place on two buttered baking sheets and proof as instructed for Soft Dinner Rolls. Preheat the oven to 425°F.
• Glaze and top the rolls as you prefer (see pages 58–61). Bake for 15–20 minutes.

BOW KNOT ROLL

SNAIL ROLL

CLOVERLEAF ROLL

TWIST ROLL

PARTYBROT

GERMAN PARTY BREAD

This German party bread makes a delicious and decorative centerpiece for any occasion that requires feeding and pleasing a crowd. These classic dinner rolls are baked together in a round cake pan and can be sprinkled with the topping of your choice (*see pages 60–61*). The dough used to make this bread is the same as that used in the recipe for Parker House Rolls.

INGREDIENTS

1 quantity dough
(see Parker House Rolls, page 118)

unsalted butter, melted, to grease pan

for the topping

egg glaze, made with 1 egg yolk and 1 tbsp milk (see page 58)

1 tbsp each sesame seeds and poppy seeds

1 Make the dough as directed in the recipe for Parker House Rolls (*see page 118*) up to step 5.

2 Divide the dough into 19 equal pieces. Shape each piece of dough into a smooth ball (*see page 55*). Grease a round cake pan or springform pan, about 9½ inches in diameter, with the melted butter.

3 Arrange the shaped rolls in the prepared pan by making an outer ring of 12 rolls and an inner ring of six rolls, and placing the last roll in the center of the two rings.

4 Cover the pan with a dish towel, then proof until doubled in size, about 45 minutes.

5 **To make the topping** Brush the top of each roll with the egg glaze, and sprinkle alternately with the sesame and poppy seeds.

6 Bake in the preheated oven for 45 minutes, until golden and hollow sounding when tapped. Turn out onto a wire rack to cool slighty, then wrap in a dish towel to keep warm. Serve immediately.

 Rising
1–1½ hours
(*see pages 50–51*)

 Proofing
45 minutes
(*see page 57*)

 Oven temperature
400°F

 Baking
45 minutes

 Yield
19 rolls

 Yeast alternative
1 cake (0.6oz) yeast
(*see page 41*)

FAN TANS

DECORATIVE BUTTERMILK ROLLS

These pretty, dainty rolls make perfect party fare. A specialty of New England, they are sometimes called Yankee Buttermilk Rolls. If you do not have any buttermilk in the house, refer to the Glossary on page 164 for a suggested substitution. The fancy shape of the rolls is easy to replicate when you follow the steps illustrated at the bottom of the page.

INGREDIENTS

2 tsp dry yeast

½ tsp sugar

⅞ cup buttermilk

2¼ cups bread flour

½ tsp baking soda

½ tsp salt

4 tbsp unsalted butter, melted, plus extra to grease tin

1 Sprinkle the yeast and sugar into the buttermilk in a bowl. Let stand for 5 minutes; stir to dissolve. Mix the flour, baking soda, and salt in a large bowl. Make a well in the center and pour in the dissolved yeast and 2 tablespoons of the melted butter.

2 Mix in the flour to form a soft, moist dough. Turn the dough out onto a lightly floured work surface. Knead until smooth, glossy, and elastic, about 10 minutes.

3 Put the dough in a clean bowl and cover with a dish towel. Let rise until doubled in size, about 1–1½ hours. Punch down, then let rest for 10 minutes.

4 Roll out the dough to form a 12 x 20-inch rectangle, ⅛ inch thick. Brush with the remaining melted butter.

5 Use a sharp knife to cut the buttered dough into seven strips, each about 1¾ inch wide. Place the strips in a stack, then cut the stack (see below, left).

6 Turn each piece cut side up and pinch the underside together to seal. Place the rolls in a well buttered muffin tin or bun tin (see below, right) and cover with a dish towel. Proof until doubled in size, about 1 hour.

7 Bake in the preheated oven for 15–20 minutes, until golden. Turn out onto a wire rack to cool slighty, then serve still warm.

 Rising
1–1½ hours
(see pages 50–51)

 Proofing
1 hour
(see page 57)

 Oven temperature
400°F

 Baking
15–20 minutes

 Yield
8 rolls

 Yeast alternative
1 cake (0.6oz) yeast
(see page 41)

SHAPING THE ROLLS

In step 5, place the cut dough strips on top of one another to form an even stack. Use a sharp knife to cut the stack crosswise into eight equal pieces.

In step 6, turn each piece cut side up and pinch the underside together to seal. Place the shaped rolls, pinched side down, in a buttered muffin tin.

SWEDISH DILL BREAD

This is quite simply the most wonderful accompaniment to smoked salmon. The cream cheese, butter, and egg produce a bread with a moist crumb, a light texture subtly scented with dill, and a golden crust studded with toasted onion.

INGREDIENTS

2 tsp dry yeast

½ cup water

3¾ cups bread flour

1 tsp salt

2 tbsp chopped fresh dill

⅔ cup cream cheese, at room temperature

2 onions, roughly chopped

2 tbsp unsalted butter, softened, plus extra to grease pan

1 egg, beaten

1 Sprinkle the yeast into the water in a bowl. Let stand for 5 minutes; stir to dissolve. Mix the flour and salt in a large bowl.

2 Make a well in the center and add the dill, cream cheese, onions, butter, egg, and dissolved yeast. Use a wooden spoon to mix all the ingredients with the flour to form a stiff, sticky dough.

3 Turn the dough out onto a lightly floured work surface. Knead the dough until silky and elastic, about 10 minutes.

4 Put the dough in a clean bowl and cover with a dish towel. Let rise until doubled in size, about 1½ hours.

5 Grease a 9 x 5 x 3-inch loaf pan with butter. Punch down the dough, then let rest for 10 minutes.

6 Shape the dough for a loaf pan (*see page 53*). Place seam side down in the prepared pan and cover with a dish towel. Proof the dough until it is ½ inch above the top of the pan, about 1½ hours.

7 Bake in the preheated oven for 45 minutes–1 hour, until hollow sounding when tapped underneath. Turn out onto a wire rack to cool.

 Rising
1½ hours
(*see pages 50–51*)

 Proofing
1½ hours
(*see page 57*)

 Oven temperature
350°F

 Baking
45 minutes–1 hour

 Yield
1 loaf

 Yeast alternative
1 cake (0.6oz) yeast
(*see page 41*)

CINNAMON RAISIN BREAD

When sliced and toasted, this bread is perhaps North America's favorite breakfast loaf—a great accompaniment to a weekend breakfast of eggs, bacon, and freshly squeezed orange juice. Any leftover slices make the perfect ingredient for another weekend breakfast favorite— French Toast, or Pain Perdu (see page 158).

INGREDIENTS

½ cup dark brown sugar

¾ cup plus 2 tbsp milk

2 tsp dry yeast

3¼ cups bread flour

1½ tsp salt

2 tsp ground cinnamon

2 eggs, beaten

3 tbsp butter, plus extra to grease pan

1 packed cup raisins

egg glaze, made with 1 egg yolk and 1 tbsp water (see page 58)

1 Add the dark brown sugar to ½ cup of the milk in a bowl. Stir to dissolve completely. Sprinkle the yeast into the milk. Let stand for 5 minutes; stir to dissolve.

2 Mix the flour, salt, and cinnamon in a large bowl. Make a well in the center and add the dissolved yeast, beaten eggs, and melted butter.

3 Mix in the flour. Stir in the remaining milk, as needed, to form a moist, sticky dough.

4 Turn the dough out onto a lightly floured work surface. Knead until smooth, soft, and supple, about 10 minutes.

5 Put the dough in a clean bowl and cover with a dish towel. Let rise until doubled in size, about 1–1½ hours.

6 Grease a 9 x 5 x 3-inch loaf pan. Punch down the dough, then let rest for 10 minutes.

7 Roll out the dough on a lightly floured work surface to form an 8 x 12-inch rectangle. Sprinkle with the raisins, pressing them down lightly into the dough.

8 Roll the dough tightly like a Swiss roll. Pinch the seam to seal. Place in the loaf pan with the ends underneath (see page 53). Cover with a dish towel and proof the dough until it is ½ inch above the top of the pan, 30–45 minutes.

9 Brush the loaf with the egg glaze and bake in the preheated oven for 45 minutes, then reduce the oven to 350°F and bake for 30 minutes more, until dark, shiny, and hollow sounding when tapped underneath. Turn out onto a wire rack to cool.

Rising
1–1½ hours
(see pages 50–51)

Proofing
30–45 minutes
(see page 57)

Oven temperature
400°F

Baking
1¼ hours

Yield
1 loaf

Yeast alternative
1 cake (0.6oz) yeast
(see page 41)

PRUNE & CHOCOLATE BREAD

INGREDIENTS

2½ tsp dry yeast

1½ cups water

3¼ cups bread flour

1½ tsp salt

1⅛ cups pitted prunes, roughly chopped

7oz bittersweet chocolate, roughly chopped

2 tbsp unsalted butter, softened, plus extra to grease pan

1 egg, beaten

This deeply indulgent loaf, chock-a-block with juicy prunes and melted chocolate, is superlative when served warm and cut into thick slices. The prunes and chocolate are best roughly chopped so that the bread is packed with large chunks of flavor. This sweet treat is perfect to serve with mid-morning coffee or afternoon tea. Try the Triple Chocolate and Hazelnut variation as a special treat for your favorite chocolate-lover.

1 Sprinkle the yeast into ½ cup of the water in a bowl. Let stand for 5 minutes, then stir to dissolve. Mix the flour and salt in a large bowl. Make a well in the center of the flour and pour in the dissolved yeast.

2 Mix in the flour. Stir in the remaining water, as needed, to form a soft, sticky dough.

3 Turn the dough out onto a lightly floured work surface. Knead the dough until smooth and elastic, about 10 minutes.

4 Put the dough in a bowl and cover with a dish towel. Let rise until doubled in size, about 1 hour. Grease a 9 x 5 x 3-inch loaf pan with butter.

5 Punch down the dough, then let rest for 10 minutes. Add the prunes, chocolate, butter, and egg (*see below, left*). Turn out onto a lightly floured work surface. Knead until just firm enough to shape, 1–2 minutes.

6 Shape the dough for a loaf pan (*see below, right*) and place in the prepared pan. Cover with a dish towel and proof the dough until it has risen 1 inch above the rim of the pan, about 30 minutes.

7 Bake in the preheated oven for 45 minutes, until lightly browned and hollow sounding when tapped underneath. Turn out onto a wire rack to cool.

VARIATION
Triple Chocolate and Hazelnut Bread

• Make one quantity Prune and Chocolate Bread dough up to step 5.
• Replace the prunes and bittersweet chocolate in step 5 with 8oz bittersweet chocolate, 4oz semisweet chocolate, 2oz milk chocolate, roughly chopped, and 1 cup roughly chopped, toasted hazelnuts. Add to the dough (*see below, left*).
• Shape, proof, and bake the dough as directed in steps 6–7.

 Rising
1 hour
(*see pages 50–51*)

 Proofing
30 minutes
(*see page 57*)

 Oven temperature
350°F

 Baking
45 minutes

 Yield
1 loaf

 Yeast alternative
1¼ cakes
(0.6oz-sized) yeast
(*see page 41*)

ENRICHING THE DOUGH

Use your hand to gently squeeze the prunes, chocolate, butter, and egg into the dough until they are evenly distributed and the beaten egg is absorbed.

SHAPING THE DOUGH

Follow the instructions on page 53 to gently shape the dough to fit the loaf pan. Place the dough into the buttered pan seam side down.

FLAT BREADS

F LAT BREADS WERE UNDOUBTEDLY SOME OF THE EARLIEST BREADS EVER BAKED. THEY CONTINUE TO BE PRODUCED TODAY, OFTEN SERVING AS PLATES AND CUTLERY FOR MEALS IN THEIR COUNTRIES OF ORIGIN. THEY ARE STAPLES PARTICULARLY IN THOSE PARTS OF THE WORLD WHERE FUEL FOR COOKING IS SCARCE—FLAT BREADS COOK VERY QUICKLY. MANY OF THESE BREADS ARE SHAPED WITH A ROLLING PIN. BREAD DOUGH ROLLS OUT MOST EASILY WHEN RESTED AT INTERVALS. WHEN MAKING THESE RECIPES, ROLL OUT THE DOUGH UNTIL YOU FEEL RESISTANCE, THEN TURN TO ANOTHER PIECE OF DOUGH, AND GIVE THE FIRST PIECE TIME TO REST. REPLICATE THE FIERCE HEAT OF THE CLAY OVENS TRADITIONALLY USED TO MAKE FLAT BREADS BY PREHEATING A HEAVY BAKING SHEET WHEN REQUIRED BY THE RECIPE.

LEFT **NAN BREADS WITH A VARIETY OF TOPPINGS**

NAN
PUNJABI FLAT BREAD

This teardrop-shaped, leavened flat bread originates in the Punjab region of northern India. Nan is traditionally baked by slapping the dough onto the side of a hot dome-shaped clay oven called a tandoor. The weight of the dough creates the characteristic teardrop shape. The core ingredients of this bread are yogurt and white flour, but it can be enriched with egg, decorated with seeds, or flavored with garlic, onion, or spices. An essential accompaniment to any classic tandoori meat or chicken dish, home-baked Nan is best eaten while still hot and fresh, with yogurt and Indian-style pickles and chutneys.

INGREDIENTS

2 tsp dry yeast
1 cup milk
4 cups all-purpose flour
1½ tsp salt
1 tsp sugar
3 tbsp plain yogurt
2 tbsp ghee or unsalted butter, melted

1 Sprinkle the yeast into ½ cup of the milk in a bowl. Let stand for 5 minutes; stir to dissolve. Mix the flour and the salt in a large bowl. Make a well in the center and add the dissolved yeast, sugar, yogurt, and ghee or butter.

2 Mix in the flour. Stir in the remaining milk, as needed, to form a stiff, sticky dough.

3 Turn the dough out onto a lightly floured work surface. Knead the dough until smooth, stiff, and elastic, about 10 minutes.

4 Put the dough in a clean bowl and cover with a dish towel. Let rise until doubled in size, about 3–4 hours. Punch down, then let rest for 10 minutes.

5 Divide the dough into four equal pieces. On a lightly floured work surface, roll out each piece to form a round, 6 inches across and ¼ inch thick. Pull one side to form a tear shape; stretch the dough until about 10 inches in length. Preheat the broiler on the highest setting.

6 Preheat a baking sheet under the broiler for about 2 minutes. Place a piece of dough on the hot baking sheet. Broil the dough in batches of two for about 2–3 minutes on each side, until puffy and golden.

7 Stack the grilled breads on top of one another and cover with a clean, dry cloth to keep the crusts soft and to prevent drying out.

VARIATIONS
Sada Nan
(Seeded Indian Flat Bread)
• Make one quantity Nan dough up to step 6.
• Combine 2 tablespoons poppy seeds and 1 tablespoon sesame seeds with 1 tablespoon softened butter.
• Spread each piece of dough with a layer of the butter mixture.
• Preheat the baking sheet and broil the breads as directed in steps 6–7.

Badami Nan
(Almond Indian Flat Bread)
• Make one quantity Nan dough up to step 6.
• Combine ⅔ cup blanched, sliced almonds and 1 tablespoon sesame seeds in a bowl.
• Melt 1 tablespoon butter, then brush over each piece of shaped dough.
• Sprinkle the almonds and seeds evenly over each piece and press down lightly into the dough.
• Preheat the baking sheet and broil the breads as directed in steps 6–7.

Rising
3–4 hours
(*see pages 50–51*)

Grill temperature
High

Cooking
Broil 2–3 minutes per side

Yield
4 breads

Yeast alternative
1 cake (0.6oz) yeast
(*see page 41*)

EKMEK
TURKISH COUNTRY BREAD

The Turks are great bread eaters, and Ekmek is very much a daily staple. Flattened, ridged rounds are the most common form given to this dough, but other popular shapes include egg-glazed rings and decorative plump braids, liberally sprinkled with sesame seeds or poppy seeds. This soft, oil-enriched bread is an eastern Mediterranean cousin of the Italian Focaccia. It is best eaten while still warm.

INGREDIENTS

1 tsp honey
1¼ cups water
2 tsp dry yeast
3¼ cups bread flour
1½ tsp salt
2 tbsp olive oil, plus extra to coat and glaze

1 Stir the honey into ⅔ cup of the water in a bowl, then sprinkle in the yeast. Let stand for 5 minutes, then stir to dissolve. Mix the flour and salt in a large bowl. Make a well in the center and pour in the dissolved yeast.

2 Use a wooden spoon to draw enough of the flour into the dissolved yeast to form a soft paste. Cover the bowl with a dish towel, then "sponge" until frothy and risen, about 20 minutes.

3 Pour about half of the remaining water and the olive oil into the well. Mix in the flour. Stir in the reserved water, as needed, to form a firm, moist dough.

4 Turn the dough out onto a lightly floured work surface.

Knead until smooth, shiny, and elastic, about 10 minutes.

5 Put the dough in a well-oiled bowl, turning it to coat evenly with the oil; cover with a dish towel. Let rise until doubled in size, about 1½–2 hours. Punch down, then let rest for 10 minutes.

6 On a lightly floured work surface, use your hands to flatten the dough into a round, 9 inches across and 1 inch thick. Place on a floured baking sheet and cover with a dish towel. Proof until doubled in size, about 45 minutes.

7 Brush the dough with olive oil. Use the blunt edge of a knife to make four parallel indentations across the dough, then four more indentations in the opposite direction to make a crisscross pattern, leaving a 1-inch border around the edge.

8 Bake in the preheated oven for 40 minutes, until golden and hollow sounding when tapped underneath. Sprinkle with extra oil, then cool on a wire rack.

To begin
Sponge method
Time: 20 minutes
(see page 44)

Rising
1½–2 hours
(see pages 50–51)

Proofing
45 minutes
(see page 57)

Oven temperature
425°F

Baking
40 minutes

Yield
1 loaf

Yeast alternative
1 cake (0.6oz) yeast
(see page 41)

CARTA DA MUSICA
"MUSIC PAPER" BREAD

Called Carta da Musica, *"music paper," because of the crunchy sound it makes when broken, this is the lightest and thinnest flat bread. Native to Sardinia, it has been eaten by Sardinian shepherds for centuries, for once baked, it may be stored for several weeks. If you are ambitious, try splitting each baked round in two for an even thinner result. Remove the bread from the oven and cut an incision along one edge with a paring knife. Use your hands to separate the bread into two very thin rounds, and return them to the oven on a baking sheet for 1 minute to crisp.*

INGREDIENTS

1¼ tsp dry yeast

1¼ cups water

3¾ cups bread flour

1½ tsp salt

1 Sprinkle the yeast into the water in a bowl. Let stand for 5 minutes, then stir to dissolve.

2 Mix the flour and salt in a large bowl. Make a well in the center and pour in the dissolved yeast. Mix in the flour from the sides of the bowl to form a stiff, sticky dough.

3 Turn the dough out onto a lightly floured work surface. Knead the dough until smooth and elastic, about 10 minutes.

4 Put the dough in a clean bowl and cover with a dish towel. Let rise for just 20 minutes. Lightly flour a baking sheet and place it in the preheated oven for 5–10 minutes.

5 Divide the dough into 16 equal pieces. On a lightly floured work surface, roll out the first piece of dough to form a paper-thin round, 6 inches across (*see below, left*).

6 Cover the remaining pieces of dough with a damp dish towel to prevent them from drying out. If the dough resists shaping, cover it with a damp dish towel and let it rest for 2 minutes. While the first piece rests, begin rolling out the next piece.

7 Immediately place the rolled-out dough on the preheated floured baking sheet (*see below, right*). Bake in the preheated oven for about 10 minutes, turning the risen round over once, until lightly colored and puffy. Reflour the baking sheet; repeat with each shaped dough round.

8 Remove the breads from the oven and pile them on top of one another on a wire rack. As the breads cool, they will become crisp and brittle.

Rising
20 minutes
(*see pages 50–51*)

Oven temperature
400°F

Baking
10 minutes
per bread

Yield
16 breads

Yeast alternative
¾ of a cake
(0.6oz-sized) yeast
(*see page 41*)

ROLLING OUT THE DOUGH

In step 5, use a narrow, floured rolling pin to roll out each piece of the dough into a paper-thin round. Cover with a damp dish towel and rest the dough for 2 minutes if it resists rolling out.

In step 7, lift the dough from the work surface with the rolling pin and transfer it to a preheated floured baking sheet.

PIADINA
ITALIAN FLAT BREAD

PIADINA FILLED WITH PROSCIUTTO AND BASIL

Once the everyday fare of the Romagna region, this rustic flat bread is now popular all over Italy, especially in bars, where it is usually served warm. It is eaten either as an antipasto, cut into wedges and sprinkled with olive oil and salt, or as panini, *wrapped around the filling of your choice, such as prosciutto and basil (see above).*

INGREDIENTS

2 tsp dry yeast
5 tbsp water
3¾ cups bread flour
2 tsp salt
1 tbsp olive oil
1 cup carbonated water

1 Sprinkle the yeast into the water in a bowl. Let stand for 5 minutes; stir to dissolve. Mix the flour and salt in a large bowl. Make a well in the center and pour in the dissolved yeast, the oil, and ⅔ cup of the carbonated water.

2 Mix in the flour. Stir in the reserved carbonated water, as needed, to form a firm, moist dough.

3 Turn the dough out onto a lightly floured work surface. Knead until smooth, shiny, and elastic, about 10 minutes.

4 Put the dough in a clean bowl, then cover with a dish towel.

Let rise until doubled in size, about 1½ hours. Punch down, then let rest for 10 minutes.

5 Divide the dough into eight equal pieces. On a lightly floured work surface, roll out each piece to form a round, 6 inches across and ½ inch thick. If the dough resists rolling out, let it rest for 1–2 minutes, then continue.

6 Heat a heavy frying pan or griddle over medium-low heat until very hot, about 10 minutes.

7 Place one of the dough rounds in the hot pan and prick all over with a fork to prevent air bubbles. Cook until golden brown on both sides, flipping it over frequently to avoid scorching and to aid even cooking, about 5 minutes.

8 Repeat with the remaining dough rounds as directed in step 7. Stack the rounds on top of one another and cover with a dish towel to keep soft and warm.

Rising
1½ hours
(*see pages 50–51*)

Cooking
5 minutes
per bread

Yield
8 breads

Yeast alternative
1 cake (0.6oz) yeast
(*see page 41*)

TORTA AL TESTO
"BREAD OF THE TILE"

The flat, crusty appearance of this age-old peasant bread inspired its name, testa, meaning "tile" in Italian. Torta al Testo is found almost exclusively in its native Umbria, and then usually a casa (in the home) rather than on the menus of bars or restaurants. This flat bread is usually cooled, sliced, stacked, and wrapped in foil, then filled and reheated just before serving.

INGREDIENTS
for the dough

2 tsp dry yeast
1⅓ cups water
3¾ cups bread flour
1½ tsp salt
1 tbsp olive oil

for the filling

2½ cups shredded fontina
6 cups arugula leaves
salt and freshly ground pepper

1 Sprinkle the yeast into ¾ cup plus 2 tbsp of the water in a bowl. Let stand for 5 minutes, then stir to dissolve. Mix the flour and salt in a large bowl. Make a well in the center and pour in the dissolved yeast and the olive oil.

2 Mix in the flour. Stir in the reserved water, as needed, to form a firm, moist dough.

3 Turn the dough out onto a lightly floured work surface. Knead until smooth, shiny, and elastic, about 10 minutes.

4 Put the dough in a clean bowl; cover with a dish towel. Let rise until doubled in size, about 30 minutes. Punch down, then let rest for 10 minutes.

5 Divide the dough into eight pieces. On a lightly floured work surface, roll out each piece of dough to form a round, 8 inches across and ¼ inch thick. If the dough resists rolling out, let it rest for 1–2 minutes, then continue.

6 Heat a heavy frying pan or griddle over medium-low heat until very hot, about 10 minutes.

7 Place one of the dough rounds in the hot pan and prick all over with a fork to prevent air bubbles. Cook until golden on both sides, flipping it over frequently to avoid scorching and to aid even cooking, about 5 minutes. Repeat with the remaining dough rounds.

8 Stack the rounds on top of one another and cover with a dish towel to keep soft and warm. When the breads are cool enough to handle, use a sharp knife to cut around the edge of each and, using your hands, divide it in half. Top one half of each bread with fontina and arugula, and season.

9 Place the other half on top of the filling and place the stuffed breads on two baking sheets. Bake in the preheated oven for 5 minutes, until hot and the cheese has melted. Cut into wedges. Serve immediately.

 Rising
30 minutes
(see pages 50–51)

 Oven temperature
350°F

 Cooking
5 minutes
per bread,
plus 5 minutes

 Yield
8 breads

 Yeast alternative
1 cake (0.6oz) yeast
(see page 41)

PITA

MIDDLE EASTERN BREAD POUCH

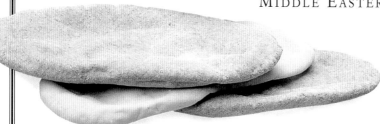

This staple bread of the Middle East, called Khubz *in Arabic, is more commonly known by its Greek name,* Pita, *in the West. Its soft, chewy crust, absorbent crumb, and hollow pouch make it the most versatile of breads, ideal to scoop up, dip in, wrap around, or be filled with all manner of food. Best served warm,* Pita *can be easily reheated: sprinkle lightly with water and warm in the oven. Keep* Pita *in a sealed plastic bag to prevent dryness.*

INGREDIENTS

2 tsp dry yeast
½ tsp sugar
1¼ cups water
3¾ cups bread flour
1 tsp salt
2 tbsp olive oil

1 Sprinkle the yeast and sugar into ½ cup of the water in a bowl. Let stand for 5 minutes; stir to dissolve. Mix the flour and salt in a large bowl. Make a well in the center and pour in the dissolved yeast and the olive oil.

2 Mix in the flour. Stir in the remaining water, as needed, to form a firm, soft dough.

3 Turn the dough out onto a lightly floured work surface. Knead until smooth, supple, and elastic, about 15 minutes. Initially, the dough will be quite stiff. It will soften and stretch gradually as you continue kneading.

4 Put the dough in an oiled bowl, turning it to coat evenly with the oil, and cover with a dish towel. Let rise until doubled in size, about 1½ hours. Punch down, then let rest for 10 minutes.

5 Divide the dough into eight pieces. Shape each piece into a smooth ball (*see page 55*). On a lightly floured work surface, roll out each ball to form an oval, 9 inches long and ¼ inch thick.

6 Cover with a dish towel and proof until slightly risen, about 20 minutes.

7 Dust two baking sheets with flour and preheat in the oven for 5 minutes. Place the dough ovals on the hot baking sheets and return immediately to the oven. Bake for 5–10 minutes until puffy. Wrap in a clean, dry cloth to keep the crusts soft and to prevent drying out.

VARIATIONS
Whole-wheat Pita
• Make one quantity Pita dough, replacing the bread flour with ¾ cup plus 2 tablespoons whole-wheat flour and 2¾ cups bread flour.
• Continue with the recipe as directed in steps 3–7.

Lavash
(Armenian Flat Bread)
(*see page 22 for illustration*)
• Make one quantity Pita dough up to step 5.
• Divide the dough into eight pieces. Shape each piece into a smooth ball (*see page 55*). Roll out each piece of dough on a lightly floured work surface to form a very thin round, about 12 inches across.
• If the dough resists rolling out, let it rest for 1–2 minutes, then continue. Cover the breads with a dish towel and proof for 20 minutes. Preheat the oven to 425°F.
• Dust two baking sheets with flour and preheat in the oven for 5 minutes. Bake the shaped dough pieces for 2–5 minutes per batch, until puffy and lightly colored.
• Wrap in a clean, dry cloth to keep the crusts soft and to prevent the breads from drying out.

 Rising
1½ hours
(*see pages 50–51*)

 Proofing
20 minutes
(*see page 57*)

 Oven temperature
425°F

 Baking
5–10 minutes

 Yield
8 breads

 Yeast alternative
1 cake (0.6oz) yeast
(*see page 41*)

PAIN TUNISIEN
TUNISIAN SEMOLINA AND OLIVE OIL BREAD

This golden, seeded bread is made with fine semolina, ground from North African durum wheat, which is also used to make couscous, the staple grain of the region. The soft, absorbent crumb is especially suited to soaking up the rich, spicy sauces of tagines, the full-flavored, slow-simmered stews of northern Africa. This bread is perhaps best enjoyed as the heart of a simple meal, served with a bowl of olives, a few dates, and a plate of cubed white cheese.

INGREDIENTS

2 tsp dry yeast

¾ cup water

1½ cups semolina

2 cups bread flour

1½ tsp salt

½ cup olive oil

egg glaze, made with 1 egg yolk and 1 tbsp water (see page 58)

4 tbsp sesame seeds

1 Sprinkle the yeast into ½ cup of the water in a bowl. Let stand for 5 minutes; stir to dissolve. Mix the semolina, flour, and salt in a large bowl. Make a well in the center and pour in the dissolved yeast and the olive oil.

2 Mix in the flour. Stir in the remaining water, as needed, to form a stiff, sticky dough.

3 Turn out onto a floured work surface. Knead the dough until smooth and elastic, about 10 minutes.

4 Put the dough in a clean, oiled bowl, then cover with a dish towel. Let rise until doubled in size, about 1–1½ hours. Punch down, then let rest for 10 minutes.

5 Divide the dough into two pieces. On a lightly floured work surface, shape each piece into a flattened round, 7 inches across and 1 inch thick.

6 Place the dough rounds on oiled baking sheets, then cover with a dish towel. Proof until doubled in size, about 30–45 minutes.

7 Brush the tops of the dough rounds with the egg glaze and sprinkle evenly with sesame seeds. Prick all over with a skewer or toothpick to prevent air bubbles.

8 Bake in the preheated oven for 30 minutes, until golden brown and hollow sounding when tapped underneath. Cool on a wire rack, then serve immediately.

 Rising
1–1½ hours
(see pages 50–51)

 Proofing
30–45 minutes
(see page 57)

 Oven temperature
400°F

 Baking
30 minutes
Steam optional
(see page 63)

 Yield
2 loaves

Yeast alternative
1 cake (0.6oz) yeast
(see page 41)

BARBARI
PERSIAN SESAME BREAD

INGREDIENTS

1 tsp honey

1¼ cups water

2 tsp dry yeast

3¼ cups bread flour

1½ tsp salt

2 tbsp olive oil, plus extra to glaze

2 tsp sesame seeds

This light, crusty bread is Iran's favorite breakfast bread, especially when topped with crumbled white cheese and sprinkled with fresh herbs. When made with milk instead of water and sprinkled with sugar instead of sesame seeds, the breads are called Shirmal and are a much loved children's snack.

1 Stir the honey into ⅔ cup of the water in a bowl, then sprinkle in the yeast. Let stand for 5 minutes; stir to dissolve. Mix the flour and salt in a large bowl. Make a well in the center and pour in the dissolved yeast.

2 Use a wooden spoon to draw enough of the flour into the dissolved yeast to form a soft paste. Cover the bowl with a dish towel, then "sponge" until frothy and risen, about 20 minutes.

3 Pour about half of the remaining water and the olive oil into the well. Mix in the rest of the flour. Stir in the reserved water, as needed, to form a firm, moist dough.

4 Turn the dough out onto a lightly floured work surface. Knead until smooth, shiny, and elastic, about 10 minutes.

5 Put the dough in a clean, oiled bowl, turning it to coat evenly with the oil, and cover with a dish towel. Let rise until doubled in size, about 1½–2 hours. Punch down, then let rest for 10 minutes.

6 Divide the dough into four equal pieces. Shape each piece into a round, 5 inches across and 1 inch thick. Cover with a dish towel and proof until doubled in size, about 45 minutes.

7 Dust two baking sheets with flour and preheat in the oven until very hot, about 15 minutes.

8 Use your fingertips to gently press into the surface of the dough to form nine dimples, about ¼ inch deep, across the top of each round. Brush each round with olive oil and sprinkle with sesame seeds.

9 Place the shaped dough on the hot baking sheets and bake in the preheated oven for 20 minutes, until golden brown and hollow sounding when tapped underneath. Cool on a wire rack.

VARIATION
Spicy Seeded Persian Bread
• Make one quantity Barbari dough up to step 8, mixing 1 teaspoon paprika and ¼ teaspoon cayenne pepper into the flour in step 1.
• In step 8, dimple each round as instructed in the recipe.
• Brush the rounds with olive oil, then sprinkle 2 teaspoons each sesame seeds, poppy seeds, and cumin seeds evenly over the top of the four rounds.
• Preheat the oven to 425°F. Place the shaped dough on the hot baking sheets and bake in the preheated oven for 20 minutes, until golden and hollow sounding when tapped underneath. Cool on a wire rack.

 To begin
Sponge method
Time: 20 minutes
(see page 44)

 Rising
1½–2 hours
(see pages 50–51)

 Proofing
45 minutes
(see page 57)

 Oven temperature
425°F

 Baking
20 minutes

 Yield
4 breads

 Yeast alternative
1 cake (0.6oz) yeast
(see page 41)

PIDE

TURKISH SEEDED BREAD POUCH

Pide *is baked in great quantities during the holy month of Ramadan. According to the Koran, bread was sent down to earth by God's command, and this soft, seeded bread is traditionally eaten at sundown to break the daily fast. Travelers' tales of long ago tell of festive* Pide *of such huge size that no oven could hold them and they were put to bake in great, ember-filled pits. Plain* Pide*, baked unglazed and without the sprinkling of seeds, is a regular accompaniment to grilled kebabs and* köfte.

PIDE

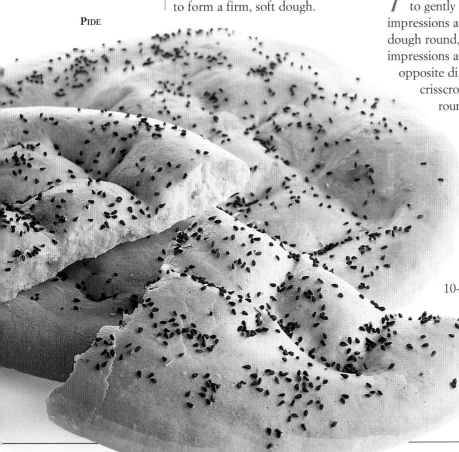

INGREDIENTS

2 tsp dry yeast

½ tsp sugar

1¼ cups water

3¼ cups bread flour

1 tsp salt

2 tbsp olive oil

egg glaze, made with 1 egg and 1 tbsp water (see page 58)

2 tsp nigella or black sesame seeds

1 Sprinkle the yeast and sugar into ½ cup of the water in a bowl. Let stand for 5 minutes, then stir to dissolve.

2 Sift the flour and salt together in a large bowl. Make a well in the center and pour in the dissolved yeast and the olive oil.

3 Mix in the flour. Stir in the remaining water, as needed, to form a firm, soft dough.

4 Turn the dough out onto a lightly floured work surface. Knead until smooth, supple, and elastic, about 15 minutes. Initially, the dough will be quite stiff. It will soften and stretch gradually as you continue kneading.

5 Put the dough in a clean, oiled bowl, turning it to coat evenly with the oil. Cover with a dish towel, then let rise until doubled in size, about 1½ hours. Punch down, then let rest for 10 minutes.

6 Divide the dough into two equal pieces. Roll each piece into a smooth ball (*see page 55*). On a lightly floured baking sheet, roll out each piece of dough to form a round, 10 inches across and ¼ inch thick. Cover with a dish towel and proof for 20 minutes.

7 Use the blunt edge of a knife to gently draw four parallel impressions across the top of each dough round, then four more impressions across the top in the opposite direction to make a crisscross pattern. Brush the rounds with the egg glaze.

8 Sprinkle the dough rounds with nigella or sesame seeds, then place them on lightly floured baking sheets.

9 Bake in the preheated oven for 10–15 minutes, until puffy and lightly colored. Wrap the breads immediately in a dish towel to keep the crusts soft and to prevent drying out.

 Rising
1½ hours
(*see pages 50–51*)

 Proofing
20 minutes
(*see page 57*)

 Oven temperature
425°F

 Baking
10–15 minutes
Steam optional
(*see page 63*)

 Yield
2 breads

 Yeast alternative
1 cake (0.6oz) yeast
(*see page 41*)

QUICK BREADS

QUICK BREADS CAN BE MADE IN MINUTES, SINCE THEY DO NOT REQUIRE THE PROLONGED KNEADING AND LENGTHY RISING ESSENTIAL FOR YEAST-LEAVENED BREADS. INSTEAD OF YEAST, THESE BREADS ARE MADE WITH A CHEMICAL RISING AGENT, SUCH AS BAKING POWDER OR BAKING SODA, THAT BEGINS TO RELEASE GAS BUBBLES THE MOMENT IT IS MOISTENED. WHEN MAKING QUICK BREADS, IT IS IMPORTANT TO BLEND THE WET AND DRY INGREDIENTS SEPARATELY AND COMBINE THEM JUST BEFORE BAKING. SWIFT, GENTLE MIXING IS ESSENTIAL BECAUSE IF THE BATTER IS BEATEN TOO VIGOROUSLY, THE GLUTEN IN THE FLOUR WILL STRENGTHEN THE MIXTURE AND THE TEXTURE OF THE LOAF WILL BE TOUGH.

LEFT **QUICK BREAD MUFFINS IN A VARIETY OF FLAVOR VARIATIONS**

CRANBERRY NUT LOAF

This festive, fruity quick bread has become a favorite Thanksgiving gift in the United States. The cranberries give the bread a juicy, tart bite that offsets the sweet, cakey crumb. This recipe can be easily adapted to make muffins as well as many other flavored loaves.

INGREDIENTS

1 tbsp oil, to grease pan

2 cups all-purpose flour, plus extra to dust pan

1½ tsp baking powder

½ tsp baking soda

½ tsp salt

½ cup pecans, coarsely chopped

1 egg, beaten

¼ cup milk

¼ cup sugar

4 tbsp unsalted butter, melted

1¼ cups fresh cranberries

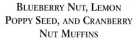

1 Grease a 9 x 5 x 3-inch loaf pan with oil. Dust generously with flour, then turn the pan to coat the bottom and sides evenly.

2 Sift the flour, baking powder, baking soda, and salt in a large bowl. Stir in the pecans and make a well in the center. Put the remaining ingredients in a separate bowl and mix until thoroughly combined.

3 Pour the mixture and the cranberries into the well. Use a spatula to gently fold all the ingredients together to form a wet batter. (Over-mixing can result in a heavy bread.)

4 Spoon the batter into the prepared loaf pan. Bake in the preheated oven for 1 hour, until golden and well-risen. The bread is ready when the edges shrink from the sides of the pan, and a metal skewer inserted into the center comes out clean.

ABOVE (FROM TOP TO BOTTOM)
BLUEBERRY NUT, LEMON POPPY SEED, AND CRANBERRY NUT MUFFINS

5 Keep the bread in the pan and let stand, about 10 minutes. Carefully run a knife around the edges and turn out. Cool on a wire rack.

VARIATIONS

Jamaican Banana Bread

• Make one quantity Cranberry Nut Loaf batter, replacing the cranberries with three ripe bananas (12oz), peeled and mashed, in step 2.
• Add ½ teaspoon ground cinnamon and ¼ teaspoon ground nutmeg to the batter in step 3.
• Spoon the batter into the prepared loaf pan as directed in step 4 and decorate the top of the loaf with ¼ cup pecan halves.
• Bake and cool as directed in steps 4–5.

Cranberry Nut Muffins

• Make one quantity Cranberry Nut Loaf batter up to step 4. Grease eight holes of a 12-hole muffin tin. Preheat the oven to 350°F.
• Spoon the batter into the muffin tin, dividing it equally among the greased holes. Bake for 15 minutes.
• Remove from the oven and allow to stand in the tin, about 10 minutes. Run a knife around the edges of the baked muffins to loosen them. Turn out, and cool on a wire rack.

Blueberry Nut Muffins

• Make one quantity Cranberry Nut Loaf batter up to step 4, replacing the cranberries with 1¼ cups fresh blueberries in step 2.
• Spoon the batter into the prepared tin as directed in the recipe for Cranberry Nut Muffins.
• Bake and cool as directed in the recipe for Cranberry Nut Muffins.

Lemon Poppy Seed Muffins

• Make one quantity Cranberry Nut Loaf batter up to step 4, replacing the cranberries and pecans with 2 tablespoons poppy seeds and the grated zest of one lemon in step 2.
• Spoon the batter into the prepared tin as directed in the recipe for Cranberry Nut Muffins.
• Bake and cool as directed in the recipe for Cranberry Nut Muffins.

 Oven temperature
350°F

 Baking
1 hour

 Yield
1 loaf

AUSTRALIAN DAMPER BREAD

Damper was the name given to the bread cooked by early settlers in Australia. The name apparently comes from the "dampening," or filling, effect it had on the appetite. Damper was originally made from just flour mixed with water, kneaded into a round, flat cake, and baked in the ashes of a campfire. Salt, milk, butter, and baking powder were added when, and if, they were available.

INGREDIENTS

2¾ cups bread flour

1 cup whole-wheat flour

4 tsp baking powder

1 tsp salt

1⅔ cups milk, plus extra to glaze

2 tbsp unsalted butter, melted

1 Sift the flours, baking powder, and salt in a large bowl, then make a well in the center.

2 Stir the milk and the melted butter together in a separate bowl. Pour the milk-butter mixture into the flour well and quickly mix in the flour from the sides of the well to form a soft, sticky dough.

3 Turn the dough out onto a lightly floured work surface. Knead the dough lightly until smooth and soft, about 1 minute.

4 Shape into a round loaf (see page 54) and place on a buttered baking sheet. Brush with milk and sprinkle with whole-wheat flour.

5 Cut a slash (see page 62), 1 inch deep, across the top of the loaf, then another in the opposite direction to make an "X."

6 Bake in the preheated oven for 15 minutes, then reduce the oven to 350°F and bake for 25 minutes longer, until golden and hollow sounding when tapped underneath. Cool on a wire rack.

Oven temperature
425°F

Baking
40 minutes

Yield
1 loaf

IRISH SODA BREAD

In Ireland, many traditional baked goods, from soda bread to scones, are made with buttermilk—the liquid left over from churning butter. If you have problems finding buttermilk, simply substitute soured milk: place 1 tablespoon of lemon juice or cider vinegar in a measuring cup and fill it up to the 1¼ cup mark with ordinary milk. This bread is best eaten on the day it is baked.

INGREDIENTS

2 cups all-purpose flour, plus extra to dust

2 cups whole-wheat flour

1 tsp baking soda

1 tsp salt

2 tbsp unsalted butter

1¼ cups buttermilk

1 Sift the flours, baking soda, and salt together in a large bowl. Rub the butter into the flour with your fingertips until evenly dispersed.

2 Make a well in the center of the mixture and pour in the buttermilk. Use a wooden spoon to stir in the flour to form a soft, crumbly dough.

3 Turn the dough out onto a lightly floured work surface. Knead very lightly until smooth, up to 3 minutes.

4 Shape into a flattened round, about 6 inches across and 2 inches thick. Dust with flour. Cut a slash (see page 62), 1 inch deep, across the top, then another in the opposite direction to make an "X."

5 Bake in the preheated oven for about 35 minutes, until hollow sounding when tapped underneath. Cover with a dish towel, then cool on a wire rack.

Oven temperature
400°F

Baking
35 minutes
Steam optional
(see page 63)

Yield
1 loaf

CLASSIC CORN BREAD

Corn bread is the original all-American bread. Recipes abound, from family to family, and from region to region, some made using white cornmeal, others with yellow, some thin, others well-risen. Out of this abundance, we chose this flavorful, enriched corn bread for its airy, slightly crunchy texture.

INGREDIENTS

2 tbsp unsalted butter, melted, plus extra to grease pan

1⅛ cups fine cornmeal

1¼ cups all-purpose flour

2 tsp baking powder

½ tsp baking soda

1 tbsp sugar

½ tsp salt

2 eggs, beaten

⅔ cup buttermilk

⅔ cup milk

1 Grease a 9-inch square, 2 inch deep, baking pan with melted butter. Place in the oven until very hot.

2 Stir the cornmeal, flour, baking powder, baking soda, sugar, and salt together in a large bowl until thoroughly combined. Make a well in the center. Whisk the eggs, buttermilk, and milk together in a separate bowl and stir in the melted butter.

3 Pour the mixture into the well, then use a spatula to gently fold all the ingredients together to form a wet batter. (Over-mixing can result in a heavy bread.)

4 Spoon the batter into the hot buttered pan—it should sizzle. Bake in the preheated oven for 20–25 minutes, until golden and well-risen. It is ready when the edges shrink from the sides of the pan and a metal skewer inserted into the center comes out clean.

5 Turn out of the pan and cool slightly on a wire rack. Cut into squares and serve warm.

VARIATIONS

Corn Sticks
(see page 21 for illustration)
Corn sticks require a special cast-iron pan with molds shaped like little ears of corn *(see page 36)*.
• Preheat the oven to 425°F. Grease the pan with oil, making sure the molds are thoroughly coated. Place in the oven, and leave until very hot.
• Make one quantity Classic Corn Bread batter as directed in steps 2–3.
• Grease the pan again with melted butter, and spoon the batter into the molds until just full.
• Bake for 15–20 minutes, until golden and the edges shrink from the sides of the pan.
• Gently ease out the sticks with a wooden skewer. Quickly rebutter the mold and bake the second batch. Serve hot or warm.

Tex-Mex Skillet Corn Bread
(see opposite for illustration)
• Preheat the oven to 425°F. Prepare a 9-inch heavy cast-iron skillet according to the instructions given for the cast-iron corn stick mold.
• Make one quantity Classic Corn Bread batter as directed in steps 2–3.
• Stir 1⅛ cups grated cheddar and two jalapeño peppers, seeded and chopped, into the batter in step 3. Continue as directed.
• Spoon the batter into the prepared skillet and bake as directed in steps 4–5.

 Oven temperature
425°F

 Baking
20–25 minutes

 Yield
1 loaf

PAIN D'EPICE
FRENCH HONEY-SPICE BREAD

This aromatic bread, with its distinctive moist honeycomb texture, dates back to medieval times. The bread improves on keeping, becoming more moist, spicy, and flavorful. For the best results, cool in the waxed paper, double wrap in foil, and store for up to three days at room temperature before eating.

INGREDIENTS

1 tbsp oil, to grease pan

1 cup honey

¼ cup dark brown sugar

1 cup whole-wheat flour

1¼ cups rye flour

2 tsp baking powder

½ tsp ground cinnamon

½ tsp ground anise seeds

¼ tsp each ground star anise, grated nutmeg, ground cloves, ground ginger

zest of 1 orange, grated

2 eggs, beaten

½ cup milk

1 Grease a 9 x 5 x 3-inch loaf pan with oil and line the sides and bottom of the pan with waxed paper. Put the honey and the sugar in a pan over low heat and stir until viscous, about 3 minutes.

2 Sift the flours, baking powder, spices, and orange zest together in a large bowl. Make a well in the center and pour in the eggs and milk.

3 Stir in the honey mixture, drawing in the flour to form a smooth batter. Pour the batter into the pan; it will be three-quarters full.

4 Bake in the preheated oven for 1¼ hours, until dark and fragrant. Because of its high sugar content, the loaf may have to be covered with foil to prevent it from burning, since the top will become very dark during cooking. The bread is ready when a metal skewer inserted into the center comes out clean. Turn out of the loaf pan, and cool on a wire rack.

 Oven temperature
425°F

 Baking
1¼ hours

 Yield
1 loaf

OLD ENGLISH CHEESE & APPLE LOAF

This moist and flavorful loaf, with its superlatively crunchy, cheesy crust, is perfect for picnics and snacks. Any apples you have on hand can be used for this recipe; however, crisp, sharp baking apples like Granny Smith are preferred.

INGREDIENTS

1 tbsp oil, to grease pan

4 cups all-purpose flour

1 tbsp baking powder

½ tsp salt

4 tbsp unsalted butter

4 apples, peeled, cored, and grated

1⅛ cups grated cheddar

2 eggs, beaten

rolled oats, to sprinkle

1 Grease a 9 x 5 x 3-inch loaf pan with oil. Sift the flour, baking powder, and salt together in a large bowl.

2 Rub the butter into the flour mixture quickly with your fingertips until the flour mixture resembles the texture of coarse breadcrumbs throughout.

3 Stir the grated apple and cheese into the flour-butter mixture. Add the beaten eggs and mix until evenly blended.

4 Spoon the batter into the prepared pan and sprinkle with oats. Bake in the preheated oven for 1½–2 hours, until golden brown and well-risen. The bread is ready when a metal skewer inserted into the center of the loaf comes out clean. Turn out of the loaf pan and let cool on a wire rack.

 Oven temperature
350°F

 Baking
1½–2 hours

 Yield
1 loaf

NUTTY YOGURT BREAD

Any well-stocked pantry should be able to provide the ingredients for this useful all-purpose emergency loaf. Quick and easy to make, this crusty loaf studded with crunchy nuts and seeds is a perfect accompaniment to a bowl of steaming soup. Delicious when served warm from the oven, it also toasts well.

INGREDIENTS

1 tbsp sunflower, extra to grease pan

3 cups flour

1 cup flour

1 tsp cream of tartar

1 tsp baking soda

1 tsp baking powder

⅔ cup mixed nuts, chopped

⅔ cup sunflower seeds

1 tsp honey

¼ cup plain yogurt

1¼ cups milk

2 tbsp sunflower seeds, to sprinkle

1 Grease a 9 x 5 x 3-inch loaf pan with oil. Sift the flours, salt, cream of tartar, baking soda, and baking powder together in a large bowl. Stir in the nuts and sunflower seeds.

2 Mix the honey, yogurt, milk, and oil. Stir into the dry ingredients and mix to form a soft dough.

3 Spoon the batter into the prepared pan and smooth to level the top. Sprinkle with sunflower seeds. Bake in the preheated oven for 1 hour, until golden and risen. The bread is ready when its edges shrink from the sides of the pan.

VARIATIONS
Seeded Yogurt Bread
• Make one quantity Nutty Yogurt Bread batter as directed in steps 1–2, replacing the nuts and sunflower seeds with 3 tablespoons each sesame and poppy seeds.
• Continue as directed in step 3. Sprinkle the top of the loaf with 2 teaspoons each sesame and poppy seeds in place of the sunflower seeds.

Herbed Yogurt Bread
• Make one quantity Nutty Yogurt Bread batter as directed in steps 1–2, replacing the nuts and seeds with 2 teaspoons dried mixed herbs (preferably *herbes de Provence*).
• Continue as directed in step 3. Sprinkle the top of the loaf with 3 tablespoons grated cheddar in place of the sunflower seeds.

Oaten Yogurt Bread
• Make one quantity Nutty Yogurt Bread batter as directed in steps 1–2, replacing the all-purpose flour with medium oatmeal and omitting the nuts and sunflower seeds.
• Continue as directed in step 3. Sprinkle the top of the loaf with 2 tablespoons rolled oats in place of the sunflower seeds.

Oven temperature
350°F

Baking
1 hour

Yield
1 loaf

FESTIVE BREADS

T RADITIONALLY, FESTIVE BREADS HAVE
PLAYED A CENTRAL ROLE IN RELIGIOUS
HOLIDAYS AND SEASONAL CELEBRATIONS.
AS A MARK OF THEIR SPECIAL, FESTIVE STATUS,
THESE BREADS ARE HEAVILY ENRICHED AND HIGHLY
FLAVORED WITH ONCE-TREASURED INGREDIENTS,
SUCH AS FRESH EGGS AND BUTTER, CANDIED FRUIT,
AND EXOTIC SPICES. MADE WITH CARE FOR SPECIAL
OCCASIONS, THE RECIPES ARE OFTEN ELABORATE
AND TIME-CONSUMING TO PREPARE. THE
TECHNIQUES DISCUSSED IN THE FLAVORED AND
ENRICHED BREAD SECTIONS, SUCH AS WORKING
IN HEAVY INGREDIENTS AND HANDLING SOFT,
BUTTER- AND EGG-RICH DOUGHS, ARE PARTICULARLY
USEFUL WHEN MAKING THESE BREADS.

LEFT **STOLLEN, THE TRADITIONAL
GERMAN CHRISTMAS BREAD**

DRESDNER CHRISTSTOLLEN
CHRISTMAS STOLLEN

A specialty of Dresden, this traditional German Christmas bread is now enjoyed around the world. The name, Christstollen, *is taken from its unusual shape—a long loaf with a ridge down the middle and tapering ends—which is said to represent the Christ Child wrapped in swaddling clothes. Traditionally, two Stollen should be baked at the same time—one for giving and one for keeping. This rich, heavy fruit dough needs an extra-large amount of yeast to rise.*

INGREDIENTS

1¼ packed cups raisins

¾ cup dried currants

¼ cup chopped blanched almonds

½ cup mixed candied peel, chopped

grated zest of 2 lemons

½ tsp ground cardamom

¼ tsp freshly grated nutmeg

pinch of black pepper

½ tsp vanilla extract

3 tbsp dark rum

6 tsp dry yeast

1 cup lukewarm milk

3¾ cups bread flour

1½ tsp salt

½ cup sugar

10 tbsp unsalted butter, softened

confectioners' sugar, for dusting

1 Place the dried fruits, nuts, peel, lemon zest, spices, and black pepper in a bowl. Pour in the vanilla extract and rum, and soak for 2 hours.

2 Sprinkle the yeast into the milk in a bowl. Let stand for 5 minutes; stir to dissolve. Mix the flour and salt in a large mixing bowl. Make a well in the center of the flour and pour in the dissolved yeast.

3 Use a wooden spoon to draw enough of the flour into the dissolved yeast to form a soft paste. Cover with a dish towel and "sponge" until frothy and risen, about 20 minutes. Add the sugar and butter to the flour well. Mix the flour in to form a soft, firm dough.

4 Turn the dough out onto a lightly floured work surface. Knead until smooth and elastic, about 10 minutes. Put the dough in a buttered bowl and cover with a dish towel. Let rise until doubled in size, about 1½ hours. Punch down, then let rest for 10 minutes.

5 On a lightly floured work surface, use the palms of both hands to flatten the dough into a square, about 1 inch thick. Scatter the fruit and almond mixture evenly over the dough and knead gently until evenly incorporated (*see page 99*).

6 Roll out the dough on a lightly floured work surface to form a flat oval, 14 inches long and 1 inch thick. Place on a buttered baking sheet. Make a lengthwise indentation down the center. Fold the dough in half lengthwise, leaving a 1-inch flap. Press the flap over to seal.

7 Use your hands to plump a small, rounded ridge down the center. Cover with a dish towel and proof until doubled in size, about 1 hour.

8 Bake in the preheated oven for 1½ hours, until firm, and a metal skewer inserted into the center comes out clean. Cool on a wire rack. Dust with confectioners' sugar, then store in an airtight container for at least a week. Serve sliced.

To begin
Sponge method
Time: 20 minutes
(*see page 44*)

Rising
1½ hours
(*see pages 50–51*)

Proofing
1 hour
(*see page 57*)

Oven temperature
350°F

Baking
1½ hours

Yield
1 loaf

Yeast alternative
3 cakes
(0.6oz-sized) yeast
(*see page 41*)

FOUGASSE
PROVENÇAL HEARTH BREAD

This branch-shaped bread forms the centerpiece of the famous thirteen desserts of Provence, which are traditional to the Reveillon *(Christmas Eve) celebrations of the region. After Midnight Mass, families return home for a glass of* vin chaud *(mulled wine) and a selection of twelve fruits, nuts, and sweets arranged around the* Fougasse, *symbolizing Christ and his apostles. Unsweetened and unperfumed, although often flavored with savory ingredients,* Fougasse *is now baked throughout the year.*

SHAPING THE DOUGH

Use your fingers to open out each slash by gently pulling the dough apart at each end.

INGREDIENTS

2 tsp dry yeast
1 cup plus 4 tbsp water
3¼ cups bread flour
1½ tsp salt
2 tbsp sugar
1 tsp anise seeds
⅓ cup olive oil
1 tbsp orange flower water

1 Sprinkle the yeast into ⅞ cup of the water in a bowl. Let stand for 5 minutes; stir to dissolve. Mix the flour, salt, sugar, and anise seeds in a large bowl. Make a well in the center of the mixture, then pour in the dissolved yeast.

2 Use a wooden spoon to draw enough of the flour into the dissolved yeast to form a soft paste. Cover the bowl with a dish towel and "sponge" until frothy and risen, about 20 minutes.

3 Add the oil and orange flower water to the flour well. Mix in the flour. Stir in the remaining water, as needed, to form a soft dough.

4 Turn the dough out onto a lightly floured work surface. Knead until smooth and elastic, about 10 minutes.

5 Put the dough in a clean, oiled bowl, turning it to coat evenly with the oil, then cover it with a dish towel. Let rise until doubled in size, about 1½ hours. Punch down, then let rest for 10 minutes.

6 Divide the dough into two pieces. On a lightly floured work surface, use the palms of your hands to flatten each piece into a tear shape, about 14 inches long and ¾ inch thick. If the dough resists shaping, let rest for 1–2 minutes, then continue.

7 Put the shaped dough on two oiled baking sheets. To form the dough into a leaf shape, make three diagonal slashes across each piece of the dough (*see page 62*). Open out each slash gently (*see below, left*).

8 Cover the shaped dough, then proof until an imprint of your finger springs back slowly (*see page 57*), about 45 minutes.

9 Bake in the preheated oven for 40–45 minutes, until crisp, golden brown, and hollow sounding when gently tapped underneath.

VARIATION
Fougasse aux Herbes (Fougasse with Herbs)

• Make one quantity Fougasse dough up to step 2, replacing the sugar, anise seeds, and orange flower water with 1 tablespoon *herbes de Provence.*
• Continue as directed in steps 3–9.

To begin
Sponge method
Time: 20 minutes
(*see page 44*)

Rising
1½ hours
(*see pages 50–51*)

Proofing
45 minutes
(*see page 57*)

Oven temperature
350°F

Baking
40–45 minutes

Yield
2 loaves

Yeast alternative
1 cake (0.6oz) yeast
(*see page 41*)

CHALLAH
JEWISH SABBATH BREAD

Egg-enriched Challah *(meaning "dough offering" in Hebrew) is usually a braided loaf. Braided* Challah *is the traditional Jewish holiday and Sabbath bread: the three strands symbolize truth, peace, and justice. A circular loaf is baked for the Jewish New Year, or Rosh Hashanah, and its round shape symbolizes continuity because it has no beginning and no end. Often* Challah *is studded with sesame or poppy seeds, which signify the manna that fell\ from heaven.*

COILED CHALLAH

INGREDIENTS
2 tsp dry yeast

¼ cups plus 2 tbsp water

3¼ cups bread flour

½ tsp salt

2 tbsp honey

2 eggs, beaten

4 tbsp unsalted butter, melted

egg glaze, made with 1 egg yolk beaten with 1 tbsp water (see page 58)

2 tsp poppy seeds, to decorate

1 Sprinkle the yeast into the water in a bowl. Let stand for 5 minutes; stir to dissolve. Mix the flour and salt in a large bowl. Make a well in the center and pour in the dissolved yeast.

2 Use a wooden spoon to draw enough of the flour into the dissolved yeast to form a soft paste. Cover the bowl with a dish towel and "sponge" until frothy and risen, about 20 minutes.

3 Add the honey, beaten eggs, and melted butter to the flour well. Mix in the flour from the sides to form a soft dough. Turn the dough out on to a lightly floured surface. Knead until smooth, shiny, and elastic, about 10 minutes.

4 Put the dough in a buttered bowl, turning to coat evenly with the butter. Cover with a dish towel. Let rise until doubled in size, about 2 hours. Punch down, then let rest for 10 minutes.

5 Divide the dough into three equal pieces. Roll out each piece to form a 16-inch-long rope. Use the flattened palms of your hands to taper the ends of each rope, so that it is thinner at both ends than in the middle, then braid the ropes (*see page 57*).

6 Place on a buttered baking sheet; cover with a dish towel. Proof until doubled in size, about 45 minutes–1 hour.

7 Brush with the egg glaze and sprinkle with poppy seeds. Bake in the preheated oven for 45 minutes, until richly golden and hollow sounding when tapped underneath. Cool on a wire rack.

VARIATIONS
Coiled Challah
• Make one quantity Challah dough up to step 5.
• Shape the dough into a long loaf (*see page 52*). Roll the dough under the palms of your hands, with even pressure, until it forms a rope, about 20 inches long. Taper the ends.
• Coil the tapered rope into a "snail"-like spiral. Pinch the end of the coiled rope to seal.
• Continue as directed in steps 6–7.

Pulla
(Finnish Crown Loaf)
(see page 18 for illustration)
• Infuse ¼ teaspoon saffron strands in ¾ cup plus 2 tablespoons heated milk.
• Make one quantity Challah dough as directed in steps 1–3, replacing the water with the milk in step 1, the honey with ⅓ cup sugar in step 3, and adding ½ teaspoon ground cardamom with the sugar to flavor the dough in step 3.
• Continue as directed in step 4. Shape the dough to braid, as directed in step 5, but do not taper the end of the ropes (*see page 57*).
• Place on a buttered baking sheet; shape the dough into a circle, and pinch the ends together to seal.
• Continue as steps 6–7, omitting the poppy seeds.

To begin
Sponge method
Time: 20 minutes
(*see page 44*)

Rising
2 hours
(*see pages 50–51*)

Proofing
45 minutes–1 hour
(*see page 57*)

Oven temperature
350°F

Baking
45 minutes

Yield
1 loaf

Yeast alternative
1 cake (0.6oz) yeast
(*see page 41*)

PAN DE MUERTO
"BREAD OF THE DEAD"

The staple flour in Mexico is cornmeal. Pan de Muerto, which is baked specially for the Mexican Day of the Dead festival, which takes place on All Souls' Day, is made instead with a highly prized ingredient: wheat flour. The bread is flavored with orange water and anise seeds and is decorated with pieces of dough that have been formed into the shape of bones. The bread is taken to the cemetery with other gifts, including chocolate, candy, and the symbolic flowers of the dead, yellow marigolds.

INGREDIENTS

2 tsp dry yeast
4 tbsp water
4 cups all-purpose flour
1 tsp salt
6 eggs, beaten
9 tbsp unsalted butter, melted
⅔ cup sugar
2 tsp anise seeds
1 tbsp orange flower water
grated zest of 1 orange
egg glaze, made with 1 egg yolk beaten with 1 tbsp water (see page 58)
sugar, to decorate

1 Sprinkle the yeast into the water in a bowl. Let stand for 5 minutes; stir to dissolve. Mix the flour and salt in a large bowl. Make a well in the center of the flour and pour in the dissolved yeast.

2 Use a wooden spoon to draw enough of the flour into the dissolved yeast to form a soft paste. Cover with a dish towel and "sponge" until frothy, about 20 minutes.

3 Add the eggs, butter, sugar, anise seeds, orange flower water, and orange zest to the flour well. Mix in the flour from the sides to form a soft, sticky dough.

4 Turn out onto a lightly floured work surface. Knead until smooth and elastic, 10 minutes.

5 Put the dough in a clean, buttered bowl, turning it to coat evenly with the butter. Let rise until doubled in size, about 2 hours.

6 Divide the dough into two equal pieces, and pinch off a quarter of each piece. Divide one of these small pieces in half and shape each one into a ball, 1 inch across. Divide the other small piece into 16 equal pieces, and shape each of them into a cylinder, ½ inch thick. Shape each cylinder into a small bone (*see below*).

7 Shape the two remaining large pieces of dough into two round loaves (*see page 54*). Place on a buttered baking sheet and stick one of the small balls on top of each loaf. Arrange the bones to form four crosses on the sides of each loaf.

8 Cover the shaped loaves with a dish towel and proof until risen, about 30 minutes. Brush the loaves with the egg glaze and sprinkle with sugar. Bake in the preheated oven for 35 minutes, until golden brown and hollow sounding when tapped underneath. Cool on a wire rack, then sprinkle with more sugar before serving.

To begin
Sponge method
Time: 20 minutes
(*see page 44*)

Rising
2 hours
(*see pages 50–51*)

Proofing
30 minutes
(*see page 57*)

Oven temperature
350°F

Baking
35 minutes

Yield
2 loaves

Yeast alternative
1 cake (0.6oz) yeast
(*see page 41*)

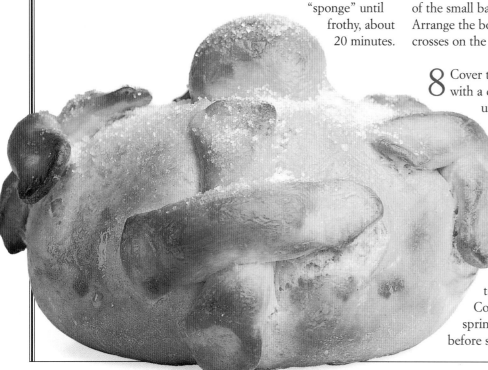

CIAMBELLA MANDORLATA
RING-SHAPED EASTER BREAD WITH NUT BRITTLE

Decorated with a crunchy-sweet nut and spice topping, this Italian Easter bread is originally from Bologna, one of the capital cities of the Emilia Romagna region. This traditional ring-shaped loaf is said to represent the unity of the family. It is now common to see the bread in Italian bakeries all year round, not just during the Easter holidays.

INGREDIENTS

2 tsp dry yeast

½ cup lukewarm milk

4½ cups bread flour

2 tsp salt

⅓ cup sugar

grated zest of 3 lemons

9 tbsp unsalted butter, softened

3 eggs, beaten

½ cup water

for the topping

4 tsp ground cinnamon

3 tbsp sugar

¼ cup blanched almonds, toasted and roughly chopped

1 egg yolk

1 Sprinkle the yeast into the milk in a small bowl. Let stand for 5 minutes; stir to dissolve. Mix the flour, salt, sugar, and lemon zest in a large bowl. Make a well in the center of the mixture and add the butter, eggs, and dissolved yeast.

2 Mix in the flour from the sides of the well. Add the water 1 tablespoon at a time, as needed, to form a soft, sticky dough.

3 Turn the dough out onto a lightly floured work surface. Knead until smooth, springy, and elastic, about 10 minutes.

4 Put the dough in a clean bowl and cover with a dish towel. Let the dough rise until doubled in size, about 4 hours. Punch down the dough, then let rest, covered with a dish towel, for about 10 minutes.

5 Divide the dough into two equal pieces and roll each piece into a 16-inch-long rope. Twist the two dough ropes together.

6 Place the dough rope on a buttered baking sheet. Shape it into a ring by bringing the two ends of the rope together. Pinch them to seal and cover with a dish towel. Proof until doubled in size, about 1½ hours.

7 **To make the topping** Mix the cinnamon, sugar, almonds, and egg yolk in a bowl. Use a rubber spatula to spread the mixture evenly over the top of the ring. Bake in the preheated oven for 45 minutes, until golden and hollow sounding when tapped underneath. Cool on a wire rack.

 Rising
4 hours
(see pages 50–51)

 Proofing
1½ hours
(see page 57)

 Oven temperature
400°F

 Baking
45 minutes

 Yield
1 loaf

 Yeast alternative
1 cake (0.6oz) yeast
(see page 41)

BOLO-REI
EPIPHANY BREAD

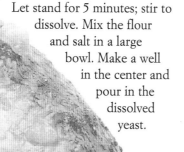

This bread, laden with nuts and glacé fruits, is traditionally eaten in Portugal to celebrate the feast of the Epiphany—when the Three Kings arrived in Bethlehem to lay their gifts at the feet of the infant Jesus. The bread must contain a bean and a gift baked inside. Whoever gets the bean is king for a day and is obliged to make the Bolo-rei next year.

INGREDIENTS

½ cup glacé citrus peel, chopped

⅓ cup each raisins and pine nuts

½ cup port

2½ tsp dry yeast

½ cup water

3¾ cups bread flour

1½ tsp salt

7 tbsp unsalted butter, softened

½ cup plus 1 tbsp sugar

zest of 1 lemon and 1 orange

3 eggs, beaten

a dried broad bean and a small present

for the topping

egg glaze, made with 1 egg yolk beaten with 1 tbsp water (see page 58)

10 glacé cherries

2 segments each glacé orange, lemon, and lime peel

sugar cubes, crushed, to decorate

apricot jam, to glaze

1 Soak the glacé peel, raisins, and pine nuts in the port overnight, or until plump and swollen. Sprinkle the yeast into the water in a bowl. Let stand for 5 minutes; stir to dissolve. Mix the flour and salt in a large bowl. Make a well in the center and pour in the dissolved yeast.

2 Use a wooden spoon to draw enough of the flour into the dissolved yeast to form a soft paste. Cover the bowl with a dish towel. "Sponge" until frothy and slightly risen, about 20 minutes.

3 Beat the butter with the sugar and the lemon and orange zest in a separate bowl until light and fluffy. Add the eggs, one at a time, and beat well after each addition. Add the mixture to the flour well, then mix in the flour from the sides to form a soft dough.

4 Turn the dough out onto a lightly floured work surface. Knead until soft, smooth, silky, and elastic, about 10 minutes. Knead in the dried fruit and pine nuts until evenly distributed (*see page 99*).

5 Put the dough in a clean bowl and cover with a dish towel. Let rise until doubled in size, about 2 hours. Punch down, then let rest for 10 minutes.

6 Shape the dough into a ring (*see page 56*), then place it on a buttered baking sheet. Wrap a dried broad bean and a trinket or small present separately in waxed paper. Insert both tiny packages into the bottom of the shaped dough.

7 Cover the dough with a dish towel and proof until doubled in size, about 1 hour.

8 **To make the topping** Brush the dough with the egg glaze and decorate with the glacé fruit and the crushed sugar. Bake in the preheated oven for 45 minutes, until golden. Warm the apricot jam in a saucepan over low heat until liquid, then brush the top and sides of the bread with it to glaze. Cool on a wire rack.

To begin
Sponge method
Time: 20 minutes
(*see page 44*)

Rising
2 hours
(*see pages 50–51*)

Proofing
1 hour
(*see page 57*)

Oven temperature
350°F

Baking
45 minutes

Yield
1 loaf

Yeast alternative
1¼ cakes
(0.6oz-sized) yeast
(*see page 41*)

PANETTONE
MILANESE CHRISTMAS BREAD

Once upon a time, a Milanese baker named Toni fell in love with a very beautiful woman who walked past his bakery every day. The baker, determined to create a magnificent bread to tempt her inside, labored for six months and finally created a tall, domed loaf that lured her in. But when their eyes met, he fell out of love with her. However, his toils were not in vain; his new creation, called Pan di Toni *("Toni's bread")—eventually corrupted to* Panettone—*is now renowned throughout Italy and the rest of the world as a favorite gift, especially at Christmas.*

INGREDIENTS

2½ tsp dry yeast

1 cup lukewarm milk

2¼ cups all-purpose flour

½ tsp salt

8 tbsp unsalted butter, softened

2 egg yolks

⅓ cup sugar

3 tbsp candied citrus peel, chopped

⅓ packed cup golden raisins

pinch of nutmeg, grated

grated zest of 1 lemon and 1 orange

1 tsp vanilla extract

egg glaze, made with 1 egg yolk beaten with water (see page 58)

confectioners' sugar, to decorate

1 Sprinkle the yeast into the milk in a bowl. Let stand for 5 minutes; stir to dissolve. Mix the flour and salt in a large bowl. Make a well in the center of the flour and pour in the dissolved yeast.

2 Use a wooden spoon to draw enough of the flour into the dissolved yeast to form a soft paste. Cover the bowl with a dish towel and "sponge" until frothy and risen, 20 minutes.

3 Mix in the flour from the sides of the well to form a stiff dough.

4 Turn the dough out onto a lightly floured work surface. Knead until smooth and elastic, about 10 minutes.

5 Put the dough in a bowl and cover with a dish towel. Let rise until doubled in size, about 1 hour. Punch down; rest for 10 minutes.

6 Grease a round mold, a deep cake pan, or a small saucepan, about 8 inches across and 6 inches deep, with softened butter. Line the base and sides of the mold with baking parchment so that it extends 5 inches above the top.

7 Knead 7 tbsp softened butter, egg yolks, sugar, citrus peel, raisins, nutmeg, lemon and orange zests, and vanilla extract into the dough until thoroughly combined, about 5 minutes (*see page 99*).

8 Shape the dough into a round loaf (*see page 54*). Place in the prepared mold. Use the tip of a sharp knife to cut an "X" across the top. Cover with a dish towel and proof until doubled in size, about 2 hours.

9 Brush the top with the egg glaze. Bake in the preheated oven for 45 minutes, until a metal skewer inserted into the center comes out clean. Remove from the mold and cool in the baking paper on a wire rack. Dust the top with confectioners' sugar to decorate.

To begin
Sponge method
Time: 20 minutes
(*see page 44*)

Rising
1 hour
(*see pages 50–51*)

Proofing
2 hours
(*see page 57*)

Oven temperature
350°F

Baking
45 minutes

Yield
1 loaf

Yeast alternative
1¼ cakes
(0.6oz-sized) yeast
(*see page 41*)

RECIPES USING BREAD

Through the ages, resourceful cooks have transformed breads into delicious sweet and savory dishes, and, although often born out of good housekeeping, many are now treasured as national favorites. These dishes usually evolved around the breads that were locally available: frugal Tuscan peasants stirred hearty country breads into soups and salads to make filling fare; thrifty British housewives incorporated pan loaves into sweet puddings; and great French chefs modeled light white breads into golden, crispy garnishes for their haute cuisine creations.

BRUSCHETTA
GRILLED COUNTRY BREAD WITH GARLIC AND OLIVE OIL

Originally a Roman specialty, Bruschetta *is now eaten throughout Italy. In Tuscany, during the olive harvest, thick slices of bread are grilled and then liberally anointed with the new season's olive oil.*

INGREDIENTS

4 slices of country bread, a day old

1 garlic clove, peeled and cut in half

4 tbsp olive oil

coarse salt

1 Toast each of the bread slices on a preheated grill (either an outdoor barbecue or oven grill).

2 While still hot, rub one side of each slice of bread with the cut side of the garlic clove.

3 Sprinkle olive oil and salt evenly over the bread slices. Serve hot. For a hearty alternative, top the grilled and seasoned slices of bread with crushed ripe tomato and freshly torn basil leaves.

 Makes
4 servings

BREADS TO USE

Broa, page 78

Pane di Semola, page 87

Pane di Prato, page 88

Pane Casalingo, page 89

Ciabatta, page 90

PAPPA AL POMODORO CON PORRI
BREAD SOUP WITH TOMATO AND LEEKS

A coarse country bread made with olive oil, such as Mantovana *or* Ciabatta, *is best suited for this hearty Tuscan soup. Although fresh tomatoes are preferable, canned tomatoes make a suitable alternative. Serve this soup with a spoonful or two of freshly grated Parmesan, a nontraditional but nonetheless delicious garnish to the recipe.*

INGREDIENTS

2 tbsp olive oil

1 onion, peeled and finely chopped

4 slim or 2 fat leeks, finely chopped

1 garlic clove, peeled and crushed

½ tsp crushed red pepper flakes

1½ lb ripe tomatoes, chopped

4¼ cups hot chicken or vegetable stock

salt and freshly ground black pepper

6 slices of country bread, a day old

6 basil leaves, torn

4 tbsp extra virgin olive oil, to serve

1 Heat the oil in a large sauté pan. Add the onion and cook over medium heat until golden and soft, about 5 minutes. Add the leeks,

garlic, and red pepper flakes. Continue to cook until the leeks are soft and wilted, about 5 minutes.

2 Stir in the tomatoes and cook until they begin to release their juices, about 5 minutes. Pour in the hot stock and bring to a boil. Season with salt and pepper and simmer gently for 30 minutes.

3 Cut the bread into 1-inch cubes. Stir the bread into the hot soup and cook for 10 minutes, until the bread is swollen and the soup has thickened.

4 Stir in the basil leaves. Check the seasoning, and add more salt and pepper if necessary. Serve in warmed bowls, with the extra virgin olive oil.

 Makes
4 servings

BREADS TO USE

Pain Ordinaire, page 72

Broa, page 78

Pain de Campagne, page 85

San Francisco Sourdough, page 86

Pane di Semola, page 87

Pane di Prato, page 88

Pane Casalingo, page 89

Ciabatta, page 90

Mantovana, page 114

PANZANELLA
TUSCAN BREAD AND TOMATO SALAD

In Tuscan farmhouse kitchens, Panzanella *is made at the end of the summer to use up the seasonal glut of tomatoes, cucumbers, and basil. In Tuscany, the bread used is* Pane di Prato, *a coarse, saltless bread, but any open-textured, country bread will do. Fresh, but very ripe, red tomatoes are essential. Let tomatoes ripen on a sunny window sill.*

INGREDIENTS

6 slices of bread, a day old

2lb fresh, ripe tomatoes, peeled and seeded

½ cucumber, peeled

1 cup black olives, pitted and halved

1 red onion, peeled and finely chopped

2 tbsp capers, rinsed

6 basil leaves, torn

⅓ cup extra virgin olive oil

2 tbsp white wine vinegar

salt and freshly ground black pepper

1 Cut the bread into ½-inch cubes and put them in a large bowl. Dice the tomatoes and cucumber and add to the bowl with the olives, onion, capers, and basil.

2 Add the olive oil and vinegar and season with salt and pepper. Stir well, then let stand for 1 hour at room temperature to allow the flavors to blend well.

3 Toss everything together thoroughly. Check the seasoning, and add more salt and pepper, if necessary, before serving.

Makes
4 servings

BREADS TO USE

Pain de Campagne, page 85

San Francisco Sourdough, page 86

Pane di Prato, page 88

Pane Casalingo, page 89

Ciabatta, page 90

PAIN PERDU
FRENCH TOAST

Pain Perdu—*literally "lost bread"—is so called because the bread is so smothered in an egg-and-milk custard that it disappears entirely, and is thus lost. In France, this favorite family leftover dish is usually served with jam, but we also love it with crispy bacon and maple syrup.*

INGREDIENTS

2 eggs, beaten

1¼ cups milk

⅜ cup sugar

8 slices of bread, a day old

8 tbsp unsalted butter

1 Place the eggs, milk, and 1 tablespoon of the sugar in a large bowl. Beat them together with a fork until thoroughly mixed and foaming. Press the mixture through a fine strainer to remove any strands of egg white.

2 Dip the bread slices into the egg mixture, submerging each slice in the egg to coat it well.

3 Melt half the butter in a large, nonstick frying pan over medium heat. When the butter begins to foam, add the slices, a few at a time, and cook until golden on both sides. Drain on paper towels.

4 Add the remaining butter to the pan as it is needed. Sprinkle the French toast with the remaining sugar immediately and serve warm.

 Makes
4 servings

BREADS TO USE

Victorian Milk Bread, page 76

Ballymaloe Brown Bread, page 78

Baguette, page 79

Brioche, page 112

Challah, page 150

BROWN BREAD ICE CREAM

A *popular dessert during the Victorian era in England, this crunchy-textured, caramel ice cream recently has been rediscovered. Brown Bread Ice Cream is best eaten when freshly made, but if you do make it in advance, remove it from the freezer and allow it to soften for 1 hour in the refrigerator before serving. Serve with raspberries and garnish with a sprig of mint.*

INGREDIENTS

2¼ cups whole-wheat breadcrumbs

⅔ cup sugar

⅓ cup water

2 cups plus 2 tbsp heavy cream

⅔ cup confectioners' sugar, sifted

1 tsp vanilla extract

2 tbsp dark rum, brandy, or whisky

1 Spread the breadcrumbs in an even layer on a baking sheet. Toast in the preheated oven, stirring occasionally, until crisp and golden brown, about 15 minutes.

2 Heat the sugar and the water in a saucepan over low heat and stir gently. When the sugar has dissolved completely to form a syrup, raise the heat and boil rapidly

until it starts to brown around the edge of the pan. Swirl the pan occasionally so that the syrup colors evenly to a rich brown. Remove the pan from the heat and stir in the toasted breadcrumbs.

3 Turn the caramel-coated crumbs out onto a baking sheet lined with baking parchment and let cool until the crumbs are hardened.

4 Wrap the baking parchment around the caramel-coated crumbs. Crush the crumbs into small pieces with your hands or rolling pin.

5 Use a hand-held mixer or balloon whisk to whip the cream until it is soft and light. Fold the confectioners' sugar, vanilla extract, and rum into the cream. Fold in the caramel-coated crumbs.

6 Spoon the mixture into a 3 cup airtight plastic container, seal, and freeze. Do not use an ice-cream machine because the churning motion will curdle the cream. Soften in the refrigerator for 1 hour before serving.

 Oven temperature
425°F

 Baking
15 minutes

 Makes
4–6 servings

BREADS TO USE

Pain Ordinaire made with brown flour, page 72

Granary Pan Loaf, page 73

Ballymaloe Brown Bread, page 78

BREAD & BUTTER PUDDING

This old-fashioned favorite was originally made with leftover plain white or whole-wheat bread, but *Victorian Milk Bread*, *Brioche*, *Challah*, and *Panettone* can be used for more indulgent versions. Try the chocolate variation for a wickedly delicious pudding. Make it with any of the breads suggested, or try it with *Cinnamon Raisin Bread* for a real treat. Soak the raisins in dark rum for a lusciously boozy twist – *Chocolate, Rum, and Raisin Bread Pudding*.

INGREDIENTS

32 Baguette slices, or 8 pan loaf slices

2 tbsp unsalted butter, softened

¾ packed cup raisins

grated zest of 1 lemon

¼ tsp ground nutmeg, plus extra to dust

3 eggs, beaten

3 tbsp sugar

2 cups plus 2 tbsp milk

½ cup heavy cream

1 tsp vanilla extract

confectioners' sugar, to dust

1 Butter the bread on one side of each slice. For pan loaf slices, cut each one in half diagonally, then into quarters. Scatter 1 tablespoon of raisins over the bottom of a buttered 1 quart oval baking dish.

2 Layer the buttered bread in the baking dish, sprinkling raisins, lemon zest, and nutmeg between each layer. Make sure that the top layer of bread is placed with the buttered side up.

3 Put the eggs and 2 tablespoons of the sugar in a large bowl. Heat the milk, cream, and vanilla extract in a saucepan over medium heat, until just boiling. Whisk the hot milk and cream mixture into the eggs and sugar to make a custard; pour over the bread. Lightly press down the bread slices to completely submerge them in the custard.

4 Dust with nutmeg and the remaining sugar. Cover the baking dish with a piece of parchment paper. Let the bread soak for 20–30 minutes.

5 Bake in the preheated oven, covered, for 20 minutes. Remove the paper from the pudding and bake for 20–25 minutes, until the custard has just set, the pudding has risen slightly, and the bread slices have turned crispy around the edges. Dust with confectioners' sugar and serve warm.

VARIATION
Chocolate Bread Pudding

• Make 1 quantity Bread and Butter Pudding up to step 2.
• Omit the lemon zest and replace the nutmeg with 1 teaspoon ground cinnamon. Arrange the bread in the dish as directed in step 2, sprinkling the raisins, cinnamon, and 3½oz bittersweet chocolate, roughly chopped, between each layer.
• Put the eggs and sugar in a large bowl. Heat the milk, cream, and vanilla as directed in step 3; remove from the heat and add 3½oz chopped chocolate. Let stand for 5 minutes, then whisk until the chocolate has completely melted.
• Whisk the chocolate mixture into the eggs and sugar, then pour over the bread. Press the bread slices down into the mixture. Omitting the nutmeg, soak, bake and serve, as directed in steps 4–5.

Oven temperature
425°F

Baking
40–45 minutes

Makes
4–6 servings

BREADS TO USE

Pain Ordinaire, page 72

Victorian Milk Bread, page 76

Ballymaloe Brown Bread, page 78

Baguette, page 79

Brioche, page 112

Zopf, page 117

Pain Viennois, page 117

Challah, page 150

Pulla, page 150

Panettone, page 155

BREADCRUMBS & CROUTONS

BREADS TO USE FOR BREADCRUMBS

•

BREADS TO USE FOR CROUTES

•

BREADS TO USE FOR DICED CROUTONS

•

BREADS TO USE FOR MELBA TOAST

•

BREADS TO USE FOR SHAPED CROUTONS

SHAPED CROUTONS

LA CHAPELURE

DRY BREADCRUMBS

The primary use of dry breadcrumbs is as a coating for ingredients to be deep-fried or roasted. Foods to be fried are usually dipped first in flour and then in beaten egg before being coated with breadcrumbs. Ingredients such as fish fillets and rack of lamb are often spread with a little smooth mustard before the breadcrumbs are pressed on. Stored in an airtight container, dry breadcrumbs keep indefinitely.

Makes 2 cups dry breadcrumbs

5 slices day-old bread, crusts cut off

Put the bread slices on a baking sheet. Leave in a 300°F oven until dry and crisp, about 10 minutes. Let cool.

To grind by hand Wrap the bread in a plastic bag. Press a rolling pin all over the bag, crushing the bread until ground to the desired consistency. Press through a strainer for a finer texture.

To grind in a food processor or blender Put the dried bread in the work bowl of a food processor or in a blender. Grind to the desired consistency.

VARIATION
Chapelure à la Provençale

• Make one quantity dry breadcrumbs.

• In a small bowl, combine the dry breadcrumbs with 2 finely chopped garlic cloves, 3 tablespoons olive oil, 1 tablespoon fresh thyme leaves, a pinch each salt and pepper, and 4 tablespoons finely chopped parsley.

• Use to coat meat or fish before sprinkling with olive oil and roasting or grilling at a high temperature.

LA PANURE

FRESH BREADCRUMBS

Fresh breadcrumbs have two main roles. In stuffings, meatloaves, dumplings, and steamed puddings, breadcrumbs bind the ingredients together. When sprinkled as a topping over gratins and other baked dishes, breadcrumbs provide both color and crunch and serve to protect creamy sauces from the high heat of the oven or grill. Fresh breadcrumbs can be stored in an airtight container and frozen for up to six months.

Makes 2½ cups fresh breadcrumbs

6 slices fresh bread, crusts cut off

To chop by hand Use a chef's knife to cut the bread into cubes on a large chopping board. Chop the bread cubes coarsely or finely as stipulated in the recipe.

To grind in a food processor or blender Cut the bread into rough chunks; put in the bowl of a food processor or a blender. Grind the bread to the desired consistency.

VARIATIONS
Panure à la Milanaise

• Make one quantity fresh breadcrumbs.

• Mix with ⅔ cup grated Parmesan.

• Use to top gratin dishes before baking or grilling at high temperature.

Buttered Crumbs

• Make one quantity fresh breadcrumbs.

• Melt 4 tablespoons butter in a pan over medium heat. When the butter is hot, add the breadcrumbs and stir well to coat evenly. Sauté until golden, about 1 minute.

• Use to top steamed vegetables.

CROUTES

Croutes *make ideal canapé bases garnished with savory toppings, like fresh goat cheese. They are also an essential component of the classic, Parisian bistro–style recipe* Soupe à L'Ognion Gratinée. Crostini *are simply the Italian (originally Tuscan) equivalent of the French* Croutes.

Makes about 32 croutes

1 day-old Baguette

Preheat the oven to 350°F.
Cut the Baguette into ½-inch slices. Place slices in a single layer on a baking sheet. Bake until crisp, about 15 minutes. Use for canapé bases or with antipasti.

VARIATIONS
Cheese Croutes
• Make one quantity Croutes as directed.
• Melt 2 tablespoons butter. Grate ⅓ cup Parmesan. Brush one side of each croute with the butter or with oil.
• Sprinkle the grated cheese and a pinch of cayenne pepper evenly over the buttered side of each croute. Place in a single layer on a baking sheet and bake until golden, 5 minutes.
• Use as a garnish for soups or salads.

Garlic Croutes
• Make one quantity Croutes as directed.
• Peel 1 garlic clove and cut it in half.
• Rub one side of each croute with the cut side of the garlic. Sprinkle this side of each of the croutes with olive oil.
• Use as a garnish for soups or salads.

DICED CROUTONS

Diced Croutons *add a delicious crunch to soups, salads, and omelettes. They are best when made just before serving, but may be prepared several hours ahead and kept at room temperature. To reheat, place in an oven, 325°F, for 5 minutes.*

Makes about 40 croutons

4 slices of day-old bread, crusts cut off

2 tbsp unsalted butter and 2 tbsp sunflower oil

To fry Cut the bread into ½-inch cubes. Heat the butter and oil in a frying pan over low heat. Test that it is hot enough by adding one cube to the pan; the bread should sizzle when it goes in. Place the croutons in the pan in a single layer. Sauté, stirring constantly, until crisp, about 10 minutes. Drain on paper towels before serving. Let cool.

Makes about 40 croutons

4 slices of day-old bread, crusts cut off

2 tbsp unsalted butter, melted

To bake Preheat the oven to 400°F. Cut the bread into ½-inch cubes; place in a roasting pan. Pour the melted butter over the cubes and toss them to coat evenly. Bake until crisp and golden, about 10 minutes.

VARIATION
Garlic Croutons
• Make one quantity Diced Croutons by either method as directed; remove from the frying pan or oven just before they are done.
• Toss with 1 finely chopped garlic clove while still hot and before draining.
• Return to a hot frying pan or oven for a couple of minutes to finish crisping.

MELBA TOAST

These *wafer-thin slices of toast make a perfect accompaniment to pâtés, smoked salmon, creamy dips, and, best of all, caviar. They can be stored in an airtight container for several days; reheat before serving.*

Makes about 32 toasts

4 slices of bread, each about ½ inch thick

Preheat the oven to 350°F.
Toast the bread slices. Cut off the crusts and slice each piece of toast in half horizontally. Cut each slice in half diagonally and in half again to make small triangles. Place on a baking sheet and bake until golden and crisp, about 10 minutes.

SHAPED CROUTONS

These *elegant, parsley-tipped shapes are used in French haute cuisine as a classic garnish.*

Makes about 12 heart-shaped croutons

4 slices of bread, each about ¼ inch thick

2 tbsp unsalted butter

2 tbsp sunflower oil

1 tbsp finely chopped parsley, optional

Cut the bread into heart-shaped pieces. Heat the butter and oil in a frying pan over low heat. Add the bread shapes to the pan in a single layer. Sauté on each side until golden, about 5 minutes. If desired, dip the pointed ends of the croutons in the finely chopped parsley.

PROBLEM SOLVING

A LESS THAN PERFECT LOAF of bread generally begins with a less than perfect dough. In fact, the most common mistake in breadmaking is producing a dough that is too dry. A dry dough is stiff and hard and will remain a solid, heavy lump that will resist proper kneading, rising, proofing, and shaping. It is impossible to specify an exact quantity of liquid or, indeed, precise rising times for each recipe when flour, temperature, and humidity vary so greatly from kitchen to kitchen, and region to region. Carefully follow the recipe instructions for dough consistency, as well as the kneading, rising, and proofing times. However, remember that bread dough is influenced by its environment. Therefore, it is important to take this factor into account and adjust the instructions as necessary. Use these guidelines to help make a perfect dough.

ACHIEVING THE RIGHT CONSISTENCY

THE IDEAL CONSISTENCY for most doughs is firm but moist. A dough should feel soft and slightly sticky after mixing, but should become smooth and elastic as it is kneaded. Resist adding extra flour until you are certain that the dough is unmanageable. Adjustments are best made at the mixing stage, but additional water or flour can be added to the dough at the kneading stage as well.

DRY DOUGH AT THE MIXING STAGE

1 The bulk of the flour and the water gather together into a ball but also leave a crumbly mass at the bottom of the mixing bowl. Add water, 1 teaspoon at a time, to the dry crumbs.

2 Use a wooden spoon to mix the dry crumbs with the water until a smooth paste is formed. Combine this mixture with the main bulk of the dough by kneading the two together with your hands.

DRY DOUGH AT THE KNEADING STAGE

THE DOUGH HAS BEEN gathered to form a ball but is still too stiff and hard to knead. Add water gradually to allow the dough to absorb the liquid without becoming a slippery, sticky mess. A water sprayer with a fine mist is best for this purpose. Spray the dough and continue kneading; repeat until you achieve the required consistency. If you do not have a water sprayer, moisten your hands lightly with water and knead. Repeat, if necessary.

WET DOUGH AT THE KNEADING STAGE

THE DOUGH IS REQUIRED to be firm enough to hold its shape after kneading. In most recipes it should become more pliable as it is kneaded: your fingers should come away as you knead, and it should feel smooth and light. However, if the dough is still too wet to work with, extra flour can be added at the kneading stage (*see right*). Dust the dough lightly with flour and continue kneading; dust again with more flour, only if necessary.

COMMON PROBLEMS IN BAKED BREADS

PROBLEM	POSSIBLE CAUSES	REMEDIES
CLOSE-TEXTURED, DENSE CRUMB	• The dough was too dry. It should feel soft and sticky after mixing. If dry, it will not develop.	• *Follow the instructions to achieve the required dough consistency given in the recipe. See instructions on the opposite page for adding additional liquid at either the mixing or the kneading stage.*
	• The dough was not sufficiently kneaded. It should feel smooth and elastic after kneading.	• *To test the dough for sufficient kneading, press it with a fingertip. The indentation should spring back immediately. If it does not, continue to knead until the dough is ready.*
	• The dough had not risen sufficiently. It should rise until it is double in volume, puffy, and aerated.	• *Check the dough after rising to be sure that it is properly risen. Use the test illustrated below to determine if more time is necessary.* • *To make sure that rising is complete, test the dough by gently pressing it with a fingertip (see right). If the dough is properly risen, it will not spring back completely. The dough will spring back at once if the rising is not complete.*
FLAT AND SPREAD-OUT LOAF	• The dough was overproofed, causing the loaf to collapse from the initial exposure to the heat of the oven during baking. When dough is very puffed up and more than doubled in volume (unless specified in the recipe), it is overproofed.	• *Punch down the shaped dough, reshape, and proof again. If the recipe requires the dough to be so soft that it does not hold its shape, use a basket to support the loaf while proofing.* • *To test the dough for overproofing, press it with a fingertip. If the dough has been overproofed, it will deflate and release a strong smell of fermenting yeast.*
CRACKS ON SIDES OF LOAF	• The dough was under-proofed, causing the loaf to expand too much in the oven. The loaf burst open during baking after the outer crust had already formed.	• *Proof until the dough has doubled in volume and is light, puffy, and aerated. Test the dough for sufficient proofing by pressing it with a fingertip. If the dough resists forming an indentation or springs back quickly, it requires more proofing time. If the indentation springs back gradually but completely, the dough is ready to be placed in the oven.*
	• The dough was improperly shaped or the seam was not sealed well at the end of shaping.	• *Review basic shaping (see pages 52–57). Be sure to always apply pressure evenly at the various steps of shaping a loaf and to allow the dough to rest between steps should it begin to resist or tighten.*
DRY PATCHES OF UNCOOKED DOUGH	• The dough was left either uncovered or in a drafty place during the rising or the proofing steps of the recipe.	• *Cover the dough securely with a dish towel (see right) and avoid drafty places. Before shaping the dough, discard any dry, crusty pieces that have formed on top.*

GLOSSARY

Anise seeds Green-brown, oval seeds with an aromatic licorice flavor. Native to the Middle East, anise seeds are widely available in most supermarkets.

Batter A mixture of flour, liquid, and sometimes leaven that can be thick or thin, but is of spooning or pouring consistency.

Biga Italian for a starter. Traditionally fermented for a minimum of 12 hours, it produces a bread with a lightly fermented taste and an open, porous texture.

Boule French for ball, referring to a round loaf of white bread also called *miche*.

Bread dough A mixture of flour, liquid, and often leaven, used to make bread. The required consistency of bread dough varies according to the recipe instructions and the desired texture and appearance of the loaf, but it should generally be stiff enough to work easily with the hands.

Brioche Traditional French bread dough enriched with butter and eggs. The classic shape, called *Brioche à Tête*, is round and has a fluted base and a topknot.

Brot The German word for bread.

Buttermilk An ingredient made by adding special bacteria to skim milk, giving it a slightly thick texture and tangy flavor. If unavailable, it can be replaced with the following mixture:
1 tablespoon lemon juice or cider vinegar, plus enough skim milk to make up
1 cup. Stir, then let stand for 5 minutes. This will yield 1 cup.

Chafe To shape a risen dough into a round by using your hands to apply a downward pressure to the sides of the dough while rotating it at the base.

Crust The hardened outer layer of, most commonly, a cooked food such as bread.

Dough A stiff but pliable mixture of flour, liquid, and other ingredients. This mixture remains a dough until it has been baked.

Fermentation A process during which carbohydrates go through a chemical change caused by enzymes produced from bacteria, microorganisms, or yeast.

Flaxseeds Also known as linseeds, these tiny, oval, shiny brown seeds are rich in nutrients and are available from health-food stores.

Ghee A concentrated, clarified butter with a strong, sweet flavor, used as a cooking fat in India and many Middle Eastern countries.

Gluten The stretchy elastic strands of protein that form when wheat flour is mixed with water and kneaded. It causes a bread dough to rise by trapping the carbon dioxide given off by the yeast and creates a network of bubbles in the crumb of the baked loaf.

Grease To prepare a bread pan or mold by brushing the inside with oil or butter before adding a dough or batter. This prevents the bread from sticking during baking.

Herbes de Provence An aromatic blend of dried herbs that grow in the Provence region of France. It usually includes thyme, rosemary, bay, basil, savory, marjoram, lavender, and fennel seeds. It is available in specialty stores and some supermarkets.

Jalapeño A dark green variety of chili that may vary from medium hot to very hot in flavor. It measures about 2 inches long and 1 inch wide, and has a rounded tip.

Key A term used to describe the final seam produced in a piece of dough once it has been folded and shaped into a loaf.

Kirsch A clear fruit brandy distilled from whole cherries. Used both as a digestive liqueur and as a flavoring in baking.

Knead To work a dough by rhythmically pushing, stretching, and folding it in order to develop the gluten in the flour.

Leaven An agent such as yeast or baking powder that is added to baked goods to lighten the texture and increase the volume.

Leavened A word describing baked goods that contain a rising agent.

Nigella seeds Available in Middle Eastern, Indian, and other specialty stores, these tiny black seeds with a nutty flavor are sometimes called black onion seeds.

Orange flower water Distilled from fresh orange blossoms, this perfumed flavoring is available in Middle Eastern, Indian, and other specialty stores.

Pain The French word for bread.

Pan The Spanish word for bread.

Pane The Italian word for bread.

Paste A mixture of flour, liquid, and sometimes leaven that is too stiff to pour, but too moist to work with the hands.

Poolish French for a starter. Traditionally fermented for a minimum of 2 hours, it produces a bread with a light, springy texture and a nutty aroma.

Proofing Also referred to as the final rise, this is the process during which a shaped dough is left to rise just before baking.

Prosciutto Also sold under the name Parma ham, this unsmoked Italian ham has been pressed, salt cured, and air dried.

Punch down To deflate a fully risen dough by pressing down on it and literally forcing the air out before the dough is shaped.

Rising The process during which a dough is aerated by carbon dioxide produced by a leavening agent before and during baking, causing it to grow in volume.

Sift To pass dry ingredients through a fine strainer in order to incorporate air and to make them lighter and more even in texture.

Slash To make incisions in the surface of a risen dough before baking to allow the loaf to rise and expand as it bakes without tearing or cracking the outer crust.

Sourdough, Sourdough bread A bread with a slightly sour, tangy flavor created by using a sourdough starter as the leaven.

Sourdough starter (*see* **Starter**) A starter that has been left to ferment for at least 48 hours. It produces a bread with a distinctive, slightly sour, tangy flavor.

Sponging The process by which a period of fermentation is added during the mixing stage, to produce a bread with a light crumb and a faintly yeasty aroma.

Star anise Available in Asian and specialty stores, this star-shaped spice has a strong, sweet aniseed flavor.

Starter A mixture of flour, yeast, and water left to ferment for 2 hours to 5 days, and up to 2 weeks. It is used as an alternative method for leavening doughs. It is added to the flour at the mixing stage when making a bread dough and affects the taste and the texture of the bread.

Unleavened A word describing baked foods that contain no rising agent.

INDEX

USEFUL ADDRESSES

UNITED STATES
Flour Suppliers/Specialty Foods
The Baker's Store (King Arthur Flour)
P. O. Box 876
Norwich, VT 05055
T: (800) 827-6836
www.kingarthurflour.com

C.F. Resources
P. O. Box 405
Kit Carson, CO 80825
T: (719) 962-3228
www.cfamilyresources.com

Crusoe Island
267 Route 89 South
Savannah, NY 13146
T: (800) 724-2233

Great Grains Milling Company
Box 427
Scobey, MT 59263
T: (406) 783-5588

Hodgson Mills, Inc.
1203 W. Niccum Avenue
Effingham, IL 62401
T: (800) 347-0105/F: (217) 347-0198
www.Hodgsonmill.com

Honeyville Grain, Inc.
11600 Dayton Drive
Rancho Cucamonga, CA 91730
T: (909) 980-9500/F: (909) 980-6503
www.honeyvillegrain.com

Kalustyan's Indian Herbs & Spices
123 Lexington Avenue
New York, NY 10016
T: (212) 685-3451/F: (212) 683-8458
www.kalustyans.com

Mountain Tops Milling
23324 Valley High Road
Morrison, CO 80465
T: (888) 303-4659
www.mountaintopsmilling.com

Pamela's Products
156 Utah Avenue
South San Francisco, CA 94080
T: (415) 952-4546

Pear Tree Specialties
P.O. Box 684
Easton, PA 18044
T: (800) 914-7063
www.pearspec.com

Stone Ground Mills, Inc.
P.O. Box 53426
Bellevue, WA 98015
T: (888) 677-3478
www.Stonegroundmills.com

Walnut Acres
Penn's Creek, PA 17862
T: (800) 433-3998

Weisenberger Mills
P. O. Box 215
2545 Weisenberger Road
Midway, KY 40347
T: (606) 254-5282

Specialty Breadmaking Equipment
The Baker's Store (King Arthur Flour)
see first entry under Specialty Flour

Bridge Kitchenware
214 East 52nd Street
New York, NY 10022
T: (800) BRIDGE-K or (212) 838-1901

Chef's Catalog
P. O. Box 620048
Dallas TX 75262
T: (800) 338-3232

Williams–Sonoma
P. O. Box 7456
San Francisco, CA 94120
T: (800) 541-2233 or (415) 421-7900

MetroKitchen, Inc.
1726 Taylor Street
Atlanta, GA 30318
T: (888) 892-3311 or (404) 367-9993
www.metrokitchen.com

Dorothy McNett's Place
800 San Benito Street
Hollister, CA 95023
T: (831) 637-6444/F: (831) 637-5274
www.happycookers.com

Pastry Chef Central, Inc.
1355 W. Palmetto Park Rd., Suite 302
Boca Raton, FL 33486-3303
T: (561) 999-9483/F: (561) 999-1282
www.pastrychef.com

**Information on Flour &
Breadmaking**
Bread Bakers Guild of America
P. O. Box 22254
Pittsburgh, PA 15222
T: (412) 322–8275

CANADA
Flour Suppliers
Rudolph Sales Inc.
1230 Old Innes Road
Ottawa, Ontario K1B 3V3
T: (613) 747-8448

Hilton Whole Grain Millers
R. R. # 2, Staffa,
Ontario N0K 1Y0
T: (800) 835-9831 or (519) 345-2582

Specialty Breadmaking Equipment
BMS Distributors
8491 Brooklyn, Kentville
Nova Scotia B4N 3W5
T: (902) 679-0008
(equipment and flour)

Ravensburg Bakery Supplies Ltd.
114–1655 Broadway Street
Port Coquitlam
British Columbia V3C 2M7
T: (604) 942-4656

Wheatland Health Kitchens Inc.
Bosch Kitchen Appliance Center
105–2800 Pembina Highway
Winnipeg, Manitoba R3T 5P3
T: (204) 275-2617

ACKNOWLEDGMENTS

AUTHORS' ACKNOWLEDGMENTS
It may take only a little time to make an honest loaf, but this book would not have been possible without the help, patience, understanding, passion, and support of a number of people.

Eric Treuille would like to thank Julia Pemberton Hellums for keeping everything together and for invaluable information about American breads and flours, Julia Brock for helping with German breads, and Didier Lascaze, my wonderful traditional baker and friend in Cahors, for helping me immeasurably to understand real breadmaking. Heidi Lascelles, who is always there for us with support, love, and enthusiasm for all enterprises at Books for Cooks, whether it be late-night recipe testing and tasting, baking workshops, or teaching nursery-school children the basics of breadmaking. Peter and Juliet Kindersley for the use of their kitchen, weekend after weekend, for bringing us back breads from their travels all over the world, and for allowing the collaboration of the "ladies" in the arduous task of quality control. The DK and studio teams for their creativity, energy, and good will in this especially challenging project. Ursula for never letting us down with her enthusiasm and

driving passion for this book and everything to do with breadmaking. Finally, special thanks to my wife, Rose, because she made this book not just possible, but the ultimate of its kind.

Ursula Ferrigno would like to thank Julia Pemberton Hellums for her outstanding editing and dedication to our book. I am thrilled for her total involvement every step of the way, and for her encouragement and persistence for a great result. Rosie Kindersley, not only for her excellent eye but also for her determination for this book to be better than any other; her researching and energy are boundless. Ian O'Leary: it has been so delightful working with him in his fabulous studio and with Emma, his assistant—his photographs are amazing. Hilary Krag and Gurinder Purewall, for their great design work. My family, as always, for their power of listening and advice and help with research. My man in Rome for just being him, and his help with my dreadful spelling. Kate O'Donnel for recipe testing so diligently in the heat of the summer. Books for Cooks for allowing me to be there for all the fun and support, particularly Heidi Lascelles, the owner. My co-author for his determination and amazing food-styling eye.

PUBLISHER'S ACKNOWLEDGMENTS
Dorling Kindersley would like to thank Neff U.K. Ltd. and Kitchen Aid for the use of their appliances, Shipton Mills for its flour and plant specimens, The Flour Advisory Board for help with flour research, Nicola Nieburg for editorial assistance, Susan Bosanko for the index, Christine Rista for picture research, and makeup artist Sue Sian.

DK Publishing, Inc., would like to thank Mary Sutherland, Joan Whitman, and, especially, Barbara Minton for testing the recipes and sharing the results.

Picture Credits
Key to pictures: t = top, c = center, b = bottom, l = left, r = right.

The publisher would like to thank the following for their kind permission to reproduce the following photographs: Musée de la Ville de Paris, Musée Carnavalet, Paris 12tl; Mary Evans Picture Library 16tl; AKG London 18tl; Dover Publications 22tl; Ann Ronan Picture Library 24tl. Photography by Ian O'Leary, except: David Murray and Jules Selmes 27c; Martin Cameron 34tr; Clive Streeter 96cl, 101r; Steve Gorton 99cl; Dave King 99cl, 115cr; Philip Dowell 144br.